George
with much love from Mother
Christmas 1982
Hartley

ROYAL HIGHNESS

SIR IAIN MONCREIFFE
OF THAT ILK, BT

ROYAL HIGHNESS

Ancestry of the

ROYAL CHILD

HAMISH HAMILTON

LONDON

to my wife Hermione

First published in Great Britain 1982
by Hamish Hamilton Ltd
Garden House 57–59 Long Acre London WC2E 9JZ

Copyright © 1982 by Sir Iain Moncreiffe of that Ilk

Book design by Patrick Leeson

British Library Cataloguing in Publication Data

Moncrieffe of that Ilk, *Sir* Iain
   Royal Highness.
   1. Great Britain – Kings and rulers – Genealogy
   I. Title
   929.7'2   CS418

   ISBN 0–241–10840–3

Typeset, printed and bound in Great Britain
by Fakenham Press Limited, Fakenham, Norfolk

CONTENTS

NOTE TO READER   In the text bold type indicates direct
ancestors and italics probable ancestors
of HRH. Direct ancestors are indicated
in the Tables by the use of capitals.

PREFACE

Mosque of the Arab Caliphs of Cordoba

A MOMENT's reflection will show that HRH's breeding is the most important in the world. Unlike most of us, whose heredity gives us what aptitudes we have, to develop as we please according to our environment, HRH is bound to a special duty by heredity from birth. So it's of more than genealogical interest to know who has gone to make it up. For HRH is at present eventual heir to the world's greatest position that is determined solely by heredity – that of Sovereign of the United Kingdom and Canada, and Head of the Commonwealth, not to mention an entire Continent 'down under'.

This breeding is changed by 50% in every generation, which is why the marriages of successive heirs to the throne are of such particular importance to us. It was not just the fairy-tale lady of his choice that Prince Charles married, but all Lady Diana's myriad ancestors who were brought into the balance too: 50% of all the royal child's genetic code. The royal stock is not chosen for musical talent (though it is there), such as was found in a long line of Mendelssohns, nor painting, which is scarcely hereditary, nor mathematical science, for which Ashkenazi Jewish genes show such a marked aptitude. From its primitive beginnings in sacral royalty, the Blood Royal everywhere has normally received a few periodic transfusions from great statesmen in peace and great commanders in war: the Princess of Wales's ancestry has these in unusual abundance. But fundamentally, our royal bloodstream is formed from the Blood Royal of the races who went to make up our United Kingdom, cross-bred with the international royalty of the other European nations who furnished ethnic groups to the Old Commonwealth. To this royal bloodstream the Princess of Wales has brought back in particular, descents from the later Royal Stuarts: King Charles I and his two sons, Charles II and James II – together with the blood of King Henri IV of France who reigned in Quebec and of the Medici of Florence – and has doubled our Royal Family's descents from the Habsburgs and the Spanish monarchs who brought about the discovery of America.

For the lines of descent set out in my Tables are usually only one selected out of many. Just as villagers before railway travel tended to marry within their own or neighbouring villages, so that on the whole they largely descended over and over again from the same group of people, thus also has Royalty always tended to marry into itself or the higher nobility – treating Europe as a village – though, since the Reformation, there has been an unfortunate tendency to divide it into two villages, the Catholic one and the rest. But, in this way, just as a particular Cornish villager will have a predominantly sturdy Cornish stock, so too, for instance, HRH has at least twenty-seven separate lines of descent from Mary Queen of Scots: twenty-two through Prince Charles and five (possibly seven) more through the Princess of Wales.

Nevertheless, it's important to emphasise that if a single one of HRH's many direct ancestors (including all those set out in heavy type in this book) – whether Alfred the Great, or the Cid, or Queen Victoria, or Earl Grey – had died in infancy, HRH could never have been born. There is no such thing as a 'tenuous' ancestry: either one descends from somebody or one does not.

For our throne passes through women; it is not with surnames and male lines that British monarchy is concerned, but with the continuing blood line of our ancient royalty. There should be no need, but in fact there is a constant need, to remind people that the Royal Family has always been the same Family, and is on the throne because of its direct descent from the Anglo-Saxon and Norman and Pictish and Scottish Blood Royal, immemorially with us since before the dawn of our national history. At this stage it may seem valid to explain

Sketch of the matrix of the seal of Kalonymos b.
Todros, last Jewish King in Narbonne c. 1280, showing
the royal lion of Judah

why the royal child is referred to throughout as
'HRH'. It's because my publishers consider that, in
order to be topically useful to the general reader, it
must go to press before the sex and name of the
child is known: but in any event, I am dealing with a
Royal Highness of the highest birth possible.

Royalty goes back to the Dawn Religion, for
sacral kingship is 'the earliest religion of which we
have certain knowledge', whereby the lucky spirit
of the community was incarnated in royalty
through inauguration rituals which scholars have
shown everywhere and at all times has contained
most of the same thirty features: among them,
anointing, prayer for special enduing with the holy
spirit, and enthronement on stone in a high place.
Thus true royalty descends from families who
embodied these communal god-spirits in pagan
times; though, as religion grew more abstract, the
spirit in the Sovereign came to be thought of as
allegorical – thus the Queen is felt to incarnate the
Spirit of Britannia. Royalty were leaders in this
transition: which can easily be studied among HRH's
ancestors who were Kings of Tara, where the
change in religion was marked by the canonisation
of nearly 300 of HRH's Ui Neill relations as Celtic
saints (see also the section on Scandinavia). Thus,
the Dawn Religion has long been secularised, but
has left a respect and a magic which has rightly
given royalty a psychological value quite apart
from government.

Indeed, it's a common mistake to dismiss kings
without political power as 'puppet kings', as
though royalty was a museum-piece left over from
brief periods of absolutism which, on examination,
prove to be the exception rather than the rule. The

Queen embodies in living flesh and blood the
'sovereign people': and it's through the formal
submission that the people insist their real rulers
make to their Queen that the people keep their end
up. 'The monarchy is not the ceremonial arm of the
government but the ceremonial arm of the
governed.'

Nevertheless, great ceremonial must be kept for
comparatively rare splendid occasions, lest fami-
liarity breeds blaséness. The other great aspect of
Royalty is that it forms the nuclear family of the
whole nation – or even, by inter-marriage, the
nuclear family that binds nations together. Indeed,
the Royal Family as an exemplar of family life is so
familiar to us that we take it for granted.

The scheme of this family book has been to set
out HRH's royal ancestry in each country, together
with descents from their other great historic
figures. For obvious reasons, it has been difficult to
venture outside Christendom, save for my agreement with Vajay's discovery of the Bassarab
dynasty's descent (and that of our **Queen Mary**)
from **Genghis Khan**. However, there are two
strong probabilities that deserve mention, since
they bear on the consecrated royalty of Ancient
Judah and on the Arab caliphs who were kindred of
the Prophet. Both cases have been under investi-
gation for some time by Professor David Kelley,
who has been most helpful although he has not yet
published his findings.

Before the expulsion of the Moors from Spain,
and the Spanish doctrine of *limpieza* or pure
Christian blood led to revision of official
genealogies, there was a tradition by 1271 (accepted
in the *Nobiliaro of Dom Pedro*, Portuguese Count of
Barcelos, in 1344) that HRH's then ancestor –
through **Blount** and **Ayala** – **Don Manrique de
Lara** was descended from *'Mudarra' Gonsalez de
Lara*, son of the marriage of *Gonzalo de Lara* to a
daughter of *Hakim II, Caliph of Cordoba* (961–76).
This Spanish oral tradition not only corresponds in
a number of important details with material from
contemporary Arab historians, but the very nickname 'mudarra' is a rare Arab name for a mule,
applied to the mixed offspring of 'good' Arabs with
other tribes. The *Caliphs of Cordoba* were
Ummayads, descended from *Hisham, 15th Caliph of
Islam* (724–43), who ruled from the borders of
China and the Indus to Spain and whose winter
palace at Jericho has been excavated: descended by
way of *Marwan, 9th Caliph* (683–5) from the senior
branch of the *Qoreish*, ruling dynasty of Mecca,
through the Prophet Mohammed's great-
granduncle *Abd Shams* the banker.

Meanwhile, the Jews in Babylonia had been administered since the time of the Captivity in the sixth century BC by their own Exilarchs or 'Princes of the Captivity' descended from King Jehoiakhin of the Royal House of David, who lived in great state in their own palace, and continued until overthrown by Tamerlane in the fifteenth century AD. The Jews of Narbonne in Septimania (now Southern France, but then under Moslem Spain) assisted the Franks to capture the city from the *Ummayad caliphs of Spain* in return for **the Frankish king** obtaining from the *Ummayads'* hereditary enemy, the Abbasid caliph of Islam at Baghdad, overlord of the Exilarchs in Babylonia, a prince of the Royal House of David to be local 'Jewish King' in Narbonne. This was done in the late eighth century, and the prince who arrived, *Makhir*, founded a line of Exilarchs in feudal France known as late as the fourteenth century as the 'Kings of the Jews' in Narbonne. In those days names were changeable between languages (just as HRH's twelfth-century ancestor **Roland, Prince of Galloway**, was called **Lochlan** in Gaelic), and it was more usual to change religion than later. Professor Zuckerman makes a good case for identifying *Makhir* with **Theuderic, Duke of Toulouse** (died 793), ancestor, in the female line of **Arnaud 'manzer', Count of Angoulême** (962–1001), himself the forefather of **Queen Isabelle of Angoulême**, mother of **King Henry III of England**: 'mamzer' is a Hebrew word denoting the offspring of a marriage between a Christian and a Jew. Thus there is an interesting probability that HRH is descended both from the *Ummayad Caliphs of Islam* and also from the *Royal House of David*.

It remains for me to express my great debt to the

Genghis Khan 'Emperor of All Men' (1162–1227)

works or thanks for the personal advice of Prince Toumanoff, Prince Schwarzenberg, Count Rüdt-Collenberg, Sir Anthony Wagner, Szabolcs de Vajay, Professor David Kelley, A. C. Addington, M. L. Bierbrier, Lindsay Brook, Dr. D. M. Dunlop, Francis Jones (Wales Herald Extraordinary), Prince Isenburg & Baron Freytag von Loringhoven, Jiři Louda & Michael Maclagan, the late Gerald Paget, Patrick Montague-Smith and David Williamson. Also, for personal assistance in enabling me to do the work, many thanks to Lachlan and Arabella Rattray of Rattray, Jane Macdonald of Clanranald and – above all – to Caroline Tonson Rye of Hamish Hamilton.

COEL HEN (*nursery rhyme Old King Coel*), *Ancient British K. Caelius Votepacus in North when Romans left Britain c.410*

VĀLA (*Princess Gwawl*), *m.* CUNEDDA, *Duke of the Britains (Gwledig), moved from north of Hadrian's Wall to drive out Irish invaders of Wales*

EINION Yrth *'the Impetuous', Prince in North Wales, at war with Gaels settled in Anglesey, 5th century*

CADWALLON *'the Long-Handed', K. of North Wales (Gwynedd), defeated Irish in Anglesey in a decisive battle*

MAELGWN *'the Tall', K. of Gwynedd (North Wales), overcame tide with a floating chair, patron of bards, d.547*

RHUN, *K. of Gwynedd, d. c.586 (half-brother of Bruide, K. of the Picts, d. c.584)*

BELI, *K. of Gwynedd, d. c.599 (named after K. Coel's legendary ancestor the god-spirit Beli Mawr)*

IAGO, *K. of Gwynedd, a benefactor of the cathedral church of Bangor, d. c.613*

CADFAN, *K. of Gwynedd, whose Latin tombstone calls him 'wisest most renowned of all kings', d.617*

CADWALLON, *K. of North Wales, overcame Northumbria, but slain 634 (m. sister of K. Penda, & dau. of* WIBBA, *K. of Mercia)*

CADWALADR *'the Blessed', K. of the Britons of North Wales, with his capital at Aberffraw, d. in great plague 664*

IDWALLON, *K. of the Britons of Gwynedd, holding also Mona (the isle of Anglesey), d. c.712*

RHODRI *Molwynog, K. of Gwynedd, whose death as 'King of the Britons' was recorded in 754*

CYNAN *of Tindaethwy, K. of Gwynedd, at war with his bro. Hywel over Anglesey, d.816*

Princess ETHYLLT, *heiress of Gwynedd, m.* GWRIAD, *Prince of Deheubarth, in male line through warrior-poet K. Llywarch* Hen *from Old King Coel*

MERFYN *'the Freckled', K. of Gwynedd, held out against all Welsh rivals & Danish Vikings, d.844; m.* NEST, *dau. of* CADELL *ap* BROCHWEL, *K. of Powys & heiress of her bro., K. Cyngen, who d.855*

RHODRI *Mawr 'the Great', K. of Wales, united Gwynedd, Powys & Deheubarth, slain by the Angles 878*

ANARAWD, *K. of Gwynedd, allied with Anglo-Saxon king* ALFRED *the Great against Danes, d.916*

IDWAL *'the Bald', K. of Gwynedd, slain 942 (his first cousin K.* HYWEL *Dda was also* HRH's *ancestor)*

Prince MEURIG, *slain 986 (when Gwynedd was conquered by his cousin K.* MAREDUDD *of Deheubarth)*

IDWAL, *claimed to be K. of Gwynedd (against* MAREDDUD*), slain 996*

IAGO III, *K. of Gwynedd, restored 1033, had skull cleft with axe by his own men 1039*

Prince CYNAN (*took refuge in Dublin during dominance of Wales by K.* GRUFFYDD *ap* LLYWELYN) *m.* RAGNHILD, *grand-dau. of* SIGTRYGG *'Silken-Beard', Norse K. of Dublin*

GRUFFYDD, *Prince of Gwynedd, restored with Norse aid, was captive of Norman–English but escaped, d.1137*

OWAIN Gwynedd, *Prince of N. Wales, 'pre-eminent above all the other princes in Wales', sent embassy to seek French aid, d.1170*

IORWERTH *'Flat-Nosed', Prince of Nanconwy, with its castle of Dolwyddelan, styled 'ruler of Arfon', 12th century*

LLYWELYN Mawr *'the Great', Prince of Wales, whose rights were secured by special clauses in Magna Carta, d. monk, 1240*

ANGHARAD *of Wales (whose bro. Gruffydd was father of Llywelyn, P. of Wales, slain 1282 & P. David, horribly executed 1283), m. Prince* MAELGWN *Fychan in Deheubarth, d.1257*

ELINOR *ferch Maelgwn Fychan, m. Prince* MAREDUDD *in Deheubarth, d.1263*

Prince OWAIN *ap Maredudd in Deheubarth, d.1275*

Prince LLYWELYN *ab Owain in Deheubarth, d.1309*

Prince THOMAS *ap Llywelyn in Deheubarth, d. c.1343*

MARGRED *ferch Thomas, m. Sir* TUDUR *Fychan ap* GRONW *of Trecastell, knight, d.1367*

MAREDUDD *ap Tudur Fychan, slew a man & fled to wild country about Snowdon*

Sir OWEN *Tudor, beheaded by Yorkists, m. secretly* CATHERINE, *Queen Dowager of England, dau. of* CHARLES VI, *K. of France*

EDMUND *Tudor, Earl of Richmond, d.1456, m. Lady* MARGARET *Beaufort, dau. of the Lancastrian leader* JOHN, *Duke of Somerset*

HENRY VII *Tudor, K. of England, abolished 'livery & maintenance' (baronial equivalent of over-mighty Trades Unions) d.1509; m.* ELIZABETH *of York (sister of Edward, P. of Wales, later boy K. Edward* V, *smothered in Tower of London)*

MARGARET *Tudor, Queen Consort of Scots (sister of Arthur, P. of Wales, & of Henry, P. of Wales, later K. Henry* VIII*)*

ancestors of HRH   *See Table 5*

BRITISH ISLES: ANCIENT BRITONS & WALES

WHEN the Romans gave up Britain in 410, the country had only been Christian for about eighty years, and it seems unlikely that the Britons were any exception to the general rule among Celtic and Teutonic peoples, that royal blood was sacred blood from pagan times. So it's not surprising that the legendary ancestor of **King Coel the Old**, whose dynasty of Ancient Britons or Cymry then appear holding the territory around Hadrian's Wall, were traced by bardic tradition to the Celtic god-spirit Beli Mawr – associated with the druids' May Day festival of Beltane, still a public holiday.

King Coel's male line formed a group of little Cymric kingdoms on both sides of Hadrian's Wall, in the area that perhaps significantly includes Arthur's Seat and Merlin's well. Later, a scion of his house became **Rhodri the Great, King of Wales** (slain 878). And descendants of **King Coel** in the female line founded the other two main royal family groups of the Cymry. One group was that which reigned over Strathclyde from Dunbarton, the *dun* or fortress of the Britons, and which included **King Ceredig** (Coroticus) to whose soldiers St Patrick wrote an angry letter because

Dunbarton, the dun or fortress of the Britons, where HRH's Ancient British ancestor King Coroticus held out in the fifth century AD

Tombstone of HRH's forefather Cadfan King of North Wales, died 617, inscribed 'Catamanus rex sapientisimus opinatisimus (most renowned) omnium regum'

while raiding Ireland they had killed some Christian converts on the very day of their baptism while still clad in white garments. HRH descends from this **King Ceredig** by way of the sister of **King Cinbelin** (Shakespeare's 'Cymbeline') and her daughter **Princess Lleian**, mother of **King Aidan of Dalriada** (slain c.608), for whom see the section on Scotland.

King Ceredig had held the office of 'Gwledig', believed to correspond with the Roman 'Dux Britanniarum' or supreme commander-in-chief in the north (and 'Count of the Saxon Shore' in the south): but the title perhaps came simply to indicate a nominal primacy amongst his fellow kings, like the equivalent titles 'vortigern' or 'riothamus' (rigotamus) applied to British high kings of the fifth century whose actual names are uncertain but were very possibly related to HRH, among them probably King Arthur. An early 'Gwledig' was **King Cunedda** (son-in-law of **Old King Coel**) who moved south from Hadrian's Wall to drive out of Wales powerful Irish settlers from Munster (whose royal family were HRH's **Eoghanachta** forefathers: see section on Ireland). Here in Wales, **King Cunedda** and his scions founded the leading royal family.

Wales itself became divided into a number of separate kingdoms, the most important perhaps being **Gwynedd** (North Wales), **Powys** (Central Wales) and **Deheubarth** (South Wales), themselves sub-divided, but whose dynasts were much inter-married: so that HRH descends from their separate royal families. However, the royal house which eventually became the most important and lasted the longest was that founded by **King Cunedda**'s line in the remote fastness of Gwynedd, and all three of the greater kingdoms were united for a while under **King Rhodri Mawr** (the Great), slain 878, of the line of **King Coel** himself: but before **Rhodri**'s time the exact pedigree is necessarily to some extent traditional.

Meanwhile, the Ancient Britons or Cymry of what is now south and eastern England were overwhelmed by the Anglo-Saxon invaders, and the retreating survivors were absorbed into the kingdoms of the Cymry in Wales (also Cornwall and Strathclyde) by the time of **Cunedda**'s famous descendant, **King Maelgwn Gwynedd** (cousin of St David but criticised by Gildas), who died in 547. His own descendant, **King Cadwallon**, nearly saved the national cause, defeating and slaying the King of Northumbria in 'the last great struggle between Briton and Englishman for supremacy in the island'; but was himself slain in 634, after which the English reached the Atlantic coast opposite the Isle of Man, and the Cymry were separated into what became Cambria (Wales) and what became Cumbria (Strathclyde).

Other famous Welsh rulers who were HRH's direct ancestors include **Hywel Dda 'the Good', King of Wales**, who codified the laws and went in 928 on a pilgrimage to Rome; **Maredudd ab Owain, King of Deheubarth** by birth and **Gwynedd** by conquest, called in the annals 'most famous King of the Britons' (died 999); **Gruffydd ap Llywelyn, King of Wales**, slain in 1063 by plotters who sent his head to the Anglo-Saxon **Earl Harold** (who afterwards fell as **King Harold** at Hastings): **Owain Gwynedd the Great, Prince of North Wales** (died 1170), who defeated **King Henry II of England** but made a wise peace with him; **'the Lord Rhys', Prince of Deheubarth** (died 1197), pre-eminent leader of the Welsh for a quarter of a century; **Llywelyn Fawr 'the Great', Prince of Wales** (died 1240), who hanged the Anglo-Norman baron **William de la Braose** for having an affair with his wife; and (through **Queen Elizabeth the Queen Mother**) that great Welsh patriot **Owen Glendower – Owain Glyndwr, last Sovereign Prince of Wales** 1403–9, who had his own Great Seal, summoned his own Parliament, held Harlech Castle, and obtained troops through an alliance with France, before being overwhelmed at last and driven to die in obscurity.

Indeed, **Owen Glendower** is to Plaid Cymru what **Hereward** was to the nineteenth-century Anglo-Saxon scholars of English liberty. Another of HRH's many Welsh forefathers of note was the famous **David Gam**, whom readers will recognise from Shakespeare as one of the few casualties on the victorious side at Agincourt. HRH's ancestral first cousin Sir Walter Raleigh tells us that when, on the eve of the battle, **Davy Gam** was questioned by the king about the numbers of the enemy, he replied that 'there were enough to be slain, enough to be taken prisoners, and enough to run away'.

Other Welsh forefathers of HRH were **Sir Rhys ap Thomas**, Knight of the Garter (died 1527), **John Trevor of Brynkinault**, **Sir John Morgan of Tredegar**, the **Herbert earls of Pembroke** and (through the present **Princess of Wales**) the **Vaughans of Trawscoed, Viscounts Lisburne,**

Great seal of HRH's ancestor Owen Glendower, last sovereign Prince of Wales 1403–6

down to the **1st Earl's** daughter, **Lady Dorothy Vaughan** (died 1849).

But their great day was in 1485, when two of HRH's Welsh ancestors together reconquered England. 'Through the instrumentality of the celebrated **Sir Rhys ap Thomas** (1451–1527), the wealthiest and the most powerful personage in South Wales, **Henry Tudor, earl of Richmond**, found the Welsh ready to rise against the usurper Richard III. With an army, largely composed of **Sir Rhys's** adherents, **Henry** was enabled to face Richard III at Bosworth, and consequently to obtain the crown of England as **King Henry VII**'. HRH's grandmother, our present **Queen**, is today the nearest Protestant heir of the Welsh **Tudor** Blood Royal.

NIALL *'of the Nine Hostages', pagan sacral K. of Tara (son of K. EOCHU 'Slaves-Lord', living 360); m. INE, dau. of DUBTACH, son of MOINDACH, K. of Ulster (with his capital at Emain Macha)*

EOGAN *'the Lion', K. of Ailech, conquered Innishowen in the North, converted by St Patrick, d.465*

MUIREDACH, *K. of Ailech, eloped with Queen EIRC (Scots wife of a British king), and d. c.480*

MUIRCHERTACH, *High-King of Tara 512–34, burnt to death by concubine avenging her father*

DOMNALL *'the Deceitful', joint High-King of Tara 563–6, supported his cousin St Columba, d. of plague*

AEDH *'of the Ague', High-King of Tara 604–12, exacted the famous cattle tribute from Leinster*

MAELFITHRIG, *K. of Ailech 628–30, killed in battle by his cousin & successor Ernaine*

MAELDUIN, *K. of Ailech 671–81, slain in battle against his kinsman rival for kingship of North*

FERGAL, *High-King of Tara 710–22, killed in battle against the Leinstermen*

NIALL *'of the Showers', High-King of Tara 763–70, abdicated, and d. a monk at Iona 778*

AEDH *'the Dignified', High-King of Tara 797–819, sent ambassadors to Emperor CHARLEMAGNE*

NIALL *'Caille', High-King of Tara 833–46, drowned trying to rescue one of his men from river Callain*

AEDH *'White-Hair', High-King of Ireland 862–79, defeated the Norse settlers in Ulster*

NIALL Glundubh *'Black-Knee', High-King of Ireland 916–19, slain in battle against Norse of Dublin*

MUIRCHERTACH *'of the Leather Cloaks', K. of Ailech 938–43, Royal Heir of Ireland, killed in battle; m. FLANN, dau. of DONNCHAD, High-King of Ireland 914–44, Head of the Southern Ui Neill*

DOMNALL *'of Armagh' O'Neill, High-King of Ireland 956–80, the first O'Neill, patron of learning*

MUIRCHERTACH *'of Meath' O'Neill, a Royal Heir of Ireland, killed in battle against Dublin Norse 977*

FLAITHBERTACH *'of the Pilgrim's Staff' O'Neill, K. of Ailech, went on pilgrimage to Rome, d.1036*

AEDH *'the Handy' O'Neill, K. of Ailech 1030–3 during his father's absence, Royal Heir of Ireland, d.1033*

DOMNALL *'the Young Ox' O'Neill, styled K. of Ulster 'with opposition', held Tulach Og, slain by his rival*

FLAITHBERTACH *'Locha Feadhaidh' O'Neill, styled K. of Ulster 'with opposition', slain by his rival*

CONOR *(Conchobar) 'of the Woods' O'Neill, styled K. of Ulster 'with opposition', slain by his rival*

TADHG *'of the Glens' O'Neill, styled K. of Ulster 'with opposition', held Tulach Og, slain by his rival*

MUIRCHERTACH *'of Moylinny' O'Neill, styled K. of Ulster 'with opposition', slain by rival though victorious*

AEDH *'the Lazy-Arsed Youth' O'Neill, K. of Cenel Eoghain 1176–7, Royal Heir of Ireland, eliminated opposition*

NIALL *'the Red' O'Neill, K. of Ulster 1230, d. by miracle after carrying off a lady from a convent; m. a dau, of CATHAL 'Red Hand' O'Conor, K. of Connaught (bro. of Ruari O'Conor, High-King of Ireland)*

BRIAN *O'Neill, last native High-King of Ireland*
1258–60, killed against the English at the
battle of Down

DOMNALL *O'Neill, K. of Ulster & Royal Heir of*
Ireland, fought for K. Edward Bruce at
Dundalk, d.1325

AEDH *'the Stout' O'Neill, K. of Ulster 1344–64,*
whose seal has his shield with the Red Hand
of Ulster

NIALL *'the Big' O'Neill, K. of Ulster 1364–94, built a*
'house for the entertainment of the literati of
Erin'

NIALL *'the Young' O'Neill, K. of Ulster 1394–1403,*
first to be styled The Great O'Neill or Ua
Neill Mor

EOGAN *O'Neill, K. of Ulster 1432–55, captured &*
mutilated three rival claimants to his throne,
d.1456

HENRY *O'Neill, K. of Ulster 1455–83, sent help to*
the Yorkists in the Wars of the Roses, d.1489

CONN *'the Big' O'Neill, K. of Ulster 1483–93,*
founded a Franciscan Friary, slain by his bro.
1493

CONN *Bacach 'the Lame' O'Neill, K. of Ulster*
1519–42, 1st Earl of Tyrone 1542–59,
subjugated by Henry VIII

FERDORCHA *(Matthew) O'Neill, 1st Baron of*
Dungannon (natural son), slain by his
lawful bro. SHANE *the Proud 1558*

Red HUGH *O'Neill, last K. of Ulster 1598–1603, 2nd*
Earl of Tyrone 1585–1608, hero of Irish
resistance, d. Rome 1616; m. SIOBHAN, *sister*
of the famous 'Red Hugh' O'Donnell & of
Ruari, 1st Earl of Tyrconell

Lady SORCHA *O'Neill, 'truly beautiful woman', m.*
ARTHUR, *1st Viscount Magennis of Iveagh,*
d.1629

Honble. EVELYN *Magennis, m. Sir* ALEXANDER
McDonnell, 1st Baronet of Moyanne, d.1634

Royal harp of HRH's forefather Brian O'Neill, last Gaelic
High-King of Ireland, killed at the battle of
Downpatrick 1260

Sir JAMES *McDonnell, 2nd Baronet of Moyanne, d.*
by 1691

SARAH *McDonnell, m.* FRANCIS *Stafford of Clonowen*

EDMUND FRANCIS *Stafford of Brownstown*

ANNE *Stafford, Viscountess Dungannon, d.1799, m.*
ARTHUR, *1st Viscount Dungannon, d.1771*

Honble. ANNE *Hill, Countess of Mornington, d.1831*

ancestors of HRH   *See next Table 3*

BRIAN *'Boru' (Boruma), High-King of Ireland, killed in victory over Norse at Clontarf 1014*

TEIGE *(Tadg) mac Briain, co-King of Munster (with his bro. Donnchad), murdered 1023*

TURLOGH *(Tairrdelbach) ua Briain, High-King of Ireland, held Court in Limerick, d.1086*

DERMOT *(Diarmaid) O'Brien, K. of Munster, d.1118 (bro. of Muirchertach, High-King of Ireland)*

TURLOGH *(Tairrdelbach) O'Brien, K. of Munster, in whose time his palace of Kincora was burnt, d.1167*

DOMNALL *Mor O'Brien, last K. of Munster, defeated Anglo-Normans at Thurles 1192, d.1194*

DONNCHAD *Cairbreach O'Brien, K. of Thomond (North Munster) 1239–42, lost Limerick town*

CONOR *'na Suidane' O'Brien, K. of Thomond, killed in battle 1258*

TEIGE *'Cael-Uisce' O'Brien, d.1259 (bro. of Brian Ruadh, K. of Thomond, torn to pieces by horses 1277)*

TURLOGH *O'Brien, K. of Thomond, d.1306*

MURTOGH *(Muirchertach) O'Brien, K. of Thomond 1311–43, in whose time English were driven from Clare*

MAHON *(Mathgamain) 'Moinnroy' O'Brien, K. of Thomond 1364–9 (bro. of K. Turlough the Bald)*

BRIAN *'of the Battle of Aonagh' O'Brien, K. of Thomond 1369–99*

TURLOGH *Bog 'the Soft' O'Brien, K. of Thomond 1446–62 (deposed his bro. K. Mahon the Blind)*

TEIGE *'an Chomhard' O'Brien, K. of Thomond, fought English, d. in his castle on Lake Inchiquin 1466*

TURLOGH *Don 'the Brown' O'Brien, K. of Thomond, 'worthy heir of Brian Boruma in war against the English' d.1528*

MURROUGH *'the Tanist' O'Brien, last K. & 1st Earl of Thomond & Lord Inchiquin, 1551 (bro. of K. CONOR: see below)*

DERMOD *O'Brien, 2nd Baron of Inchiquin, d.1552; m.* MARGARET, *dau. of* DONOUGH *O'Brien, 2nd Earl of Thomond, murdered 1553, son of K.* CONOR *O'Brien, d.1540*

MURROUGH *O'Brien, 3rd Baron of Inchiquin, d. aged 23 in 1573*

MURROUGH *O'Brien, 4th Baron of Inchiquin, d.1597*

Sacred Tara, where HRH's forebears reigned as High-Kings of all Ireland

DERMOD *O'Brien, 5th Baron of Inchiquin, d.1624*

Honble. MARY *O'Brien (sister of Murrough O'Brien,*
1st Earl of Inchiquin, French cavalry general
& Viceroy of Catalonia); m. MICHAEL
Boyle, Archbishop of Armagh, Lord
Chancellor of Ireland, d.1702

ELEANOR *Boyle (sister of Murrough, 1st Viscount*
Blesinton, of family who discovered 'Boyle's
Law' in physics), m. WILLIAM *Hill of*
Hillsborough, PC, MP, HM *Lieut. of counties*
Down & Antrim, d.1693

MICHAEL *Hill of Hillsborough,* PC, MP, HM *Lieut. of*
Co. Down, d. aged 27 in 1699

ARTHUR, *1st Viscount Dungannon, d.1771 (married*
descendant of O'Neill barons of Dungannon)

Honble. ANNE *Hill, Countess of Mornington, d.1831;*
m. GARRET, *1st Earl of Mornington, d.1781*

RICHARD, *Marquess Wellesley, Gov.-Gen. of India*
& Foreign Secretary, d.1842 (bro. of 'Iron
Duke' of Wellington)

ANNE *Wellesley (natural daughter), d.1875; m. Lord*
WILLIAM *Cavendish Bentinck, d.1826, son*
of WILLIAM, *3rd Duke of Portland,* KG,
Prime Minister

Revd. CHARLES WILLIAM FREDERICK *Cavendish*
Bentinck (whose first, childless wife was a
gypsy) d.1865

NINA CECILIA *Cavendish Bentinck, Countess of*
Strathmore, GCVO, *d.1938; m.* CLAUDE
Bowes Lyon, 14th Earl of Strathmore &
Kinghorne, KG, KT, *d.1944*

Queen ELIZABETH *the Queen Mother, b. 1900*

H.M. *the Queen, b. 1926*

Prince CHARLES, *Prince of Wales, b. 1948*

HRH

BRITISH ISLES: IRELAND

THERE were about ninety kingdoms in Ancient
Ireland, each with its sacred king, so that
everybody could know his or her own king personally. The Irish word for king is *ri*, from the same
root as Hindu *raja* and French *roi*. An Irish king
reigned over a *tuath*, a tiny nation whose 'rising-
out' might be at most a few hundred fighting men.
He was their war-leader, but had to act as a sort of
lucky mascot by avoiding certain taboos called *gessa*
and enforcing certain royal privileges called *buada*.
Thus the King of Tara could not enter North
Tethba on a Tuesday, but the hares of Naas had to
be brought to him on 1st August. Such kings were
enthroned by very ancient rituals, and indeed HRH's
ancestors who were **Kings of Cineal Conaill**
(Donegal) were inaugurated as late as the twelfth
century by the sacrifice of a white mare, going
down on all fours like a stallion and bathing in its
broth: reminiscent of the sacrifice of a white horse
at a Vedic 'wheel-king's' inauguration in Ancient
India. Indeed the prestige of a *ri* was invariably that
he was sprung from an immemorial line of sacral
kings who had incarnated god-spirits in pagan
times.

Originally, the Irish had three grades of king:
above each *ri* a *ruiri* or 'superior king', and above
each *ruiri* a *ri ruirech* or 'king of superior kings'.
These over-kings were (in historical theory) originally five in number: the **Kings of Ulster, Leinster, Munster, Connaught** – and **Meath**, the
'middle' that included sacral Tara. Later there were
more and the **Kings of Tara** gradually attained a
yet higher rank: that of *ard-ri* or **High King of all
Ireland**. There was another, and fundamental,
division of the island into the northern and southern halves.

The northern half, including the midlands, was
called *Leth Cuinn* or 'Conn's Half' because its principal dynasty, the **Connachta** (with their most
powerful branch the **Ui Neill**), descended in pagan
times from ritual incarnations of the fearsome
god-spirit 'Conn of the Hundred Battles', whose
great idol had seven-clawed talons and travelled in a
chariot with nine sacrificed captives' heads hung
from each arm. The southern half of Ireland, effec-
tively Munster, was called *Leth Moga* or 'Mug's
Half' because it was dominated by the
Eoganachta dynasty, kindest and most civilised of
Gaelic royal families, whose eponymous forefather, the sacral dynast **Eogan**, had been dedicated

The Rock of Cashel whence HRH's forebears reigned as Kings of Munster

in late pagan times to the Celtic god-spirit Nuadu by receiving the throne-name of **Mug Nuadat**, literally 'slave of Nuadu'.

The vigorous ancestors of the **Ui Neill** came bursting eastwards out of Connaught taking 'sword-land' in Meath, until by the 300s AD they had captured sacred Tara itself. These pagan Iron Age kings were associated with human sacrifice of royal victims from within their own dynastic family, for 'as in the sacred grove of the Golden Bough, the king of Tara reigned, as a rule, by virtue of having slain his predecessor'. If by mischance the king died a natural death, the druids performed a white-bull sacrifice to determine into which prince of the dynasty the lucky spirit of the Conn-folk had passed. Each king underwent the mystery of four tests, and was inaugurated to the weird sound of a bull-roarer at the celebrated *Lia Fal* or Stone of Destiny still to be seen at Tara. Irish kings were ceremonially wed to the female spirit of their country, and it is significant that the goddess-spirit both of the old **Connachta** capital Cruachain and of Tara was Medb: the 'Queen Maeve' of the fairy tale heroic sagas.

In 'Conn's Half', these **Ui Neill** took their dynastic name from **Niall of the Nine Hostages, pagan sacral King of Tara**, living AD 400. Under his sons most of the North was conquered from the ancient **Ulidian kings of Ulster**, whose famous capital at Emain Macha was destroyed, and the prehistoric drystone fortress at Ailech occupied. But the mother of **Niall of the Nine Hostages'** son **Eogan, King of Ailech**, was **Ine**, daughter of **Dubtach**, son of **Moindach, King of Ulster**, so the Blood Royal of the ancient Ulidians of the heroic age continued in the new fifth century conquerors of the North and thus down to HRH.

From Tara, the **Ui Neill** gradually claimed hegemony over all Ireland, and assumed the title of High-King; although it was not until 858 that HRH's ancestor **Mael Sechnaill, King of Tara** took hostages from the entire kingdom of Munster; and on his death in 862, the annalists called him '**King of all Ireland**'; *ri Erenn uile* – the first contemporary use of 'High-King of Ireland', the *ard-ri Erenn*, being when **King Domnall ua Neill**'s death was recorded in 980. The dynasty had long been divided into two main branches, from both of which HRH descends, the **Kings of Meath** and the **Kings of the North**, who alternated in the **Kingship of Tara** itself.

In 'Conn's Half', the biggest problem for the **Ui Neill high-kings** was originally to exact the boruma or cattle-tribute, which was never given up without a fight, from the **Kings of Leinster**: HRH's ancestors from the most ancient times by way of **Murchad, King of Leinster** 715–27, **King Diarmait mac Mail-na-mBó** (died 1072), who harried England after Hastings, the tragic **King Diarmaid** (died 1171) and **Domnall, The Mac-Murrough Kavanagh** (died 1476); and who never forgot that Tara had once been theirs. Indeed, the pagan Kings of Tara and Leinster used to be buried upright and fully armed in their own ramparts facing towards each other's citadel.

Meanwhile, in 'Mug's Half' the **Eoganachta** had established themselves as **Kings of Munster**. Their most famous early ancestor, **King Conall Corc**, was probably already a Christian, one of the Irish dynasts driven out of Wales by **Cunedda** early in the 400s, and may have founded his capital on the rock of Cashel as a Christian site before the coming of St Patrick to the northern half of Ireland. Some of the greatest Eoganachta kings were also bishops or abbots, and HRH descends from this dynasty through **Cormac Mac-Carthaigh, King of Desmond** (South Munster) 1124–31, builder of that gem of Irish architecture, 'King Cormac's Chapel' at Cashel, and **Sir Owen 'of the Parliament', chieftain of Carbery**, inaugurated as **The MacCarthy Reagh** in 1576; whose daughter's husband **Edmond Fitz-Gerald, Knight of the Valley** (i.e. **The Black Knight** or **Knight of Glin**), rebuilt Glin Castle in 1615 after it had been destroyed in the last resistance to the English.

Ireland had been subject to invasion from the earliest times, the Gaels themselves having been Iron Age invaders. In 919 the **High-King Niall Glundubh 'Black-Knee'**, from whom the O'Neill kings of Ulster took their surname, was slain in battle against the Norse sea-king *Sigtryg*

Caoch, King of Dublin, probably himself also HRH's ancestor through the **Kings of Man & the Hebrides**. As a result of this Norse presence, both the Eoganachta and the Ui Neill were weakened, and a new dynasty came to the fore: the **Dal Cais**. They were originally a minor under-kingdom, though their local kings were immemorially royal, but by 951 their **King Cenetig** died as **King of Thomond** (North Munster). His own son **Brian Boruma, High-King of Ireland**, better known as **'Brian Boru'**, and from whom the O'Brien kings and earls of Thomond took their name, was the first High-King not to be of the Ui Neill, but one of the greatest Irishmen of all time: inscribed in the *Book of Armagh* as *imperator Scotorum*, 'emperor of the Irish'. In 1014, however, his ghostly family banshee Aibhill appeared in his tent to warn him of his impending doom, and he was slain in the moment of victory over **Sigurd the Fat, Jarl of Orkney** at the battle of Clontarf.

Banshees are similar to the Norse *fylgia*, an attendant spirit, sometimes in animal form, but for a whole family often a maiden (a *ban sidhe* or white fairy): usually only seen or heard as a sign of impending doom, like Melusine. HRH's native Irish **O'Brien** and **O'Neill** ancestors had their hereditary banshees Aibhill and Mauveen; but perhaps the most weird of all were the foxes who appeared to presage the deaths of HRH's Norman-Irish forefathers the **Preston viscounts Gormanston** (whose crest is a fox), and have continued to do so for the peers of that family into this century.

After **'Brian Boru'**'s time, the **O'Conor kings of Connaught** also competed for the high-kingship: so that the later High-Kings of Ireland included HRH's ancestor **King Turlough O'Conor (Toirrdelbach Ua Conchobair**, 1121–56) and his son, the famous King Ruari O'Conor (1166–86), whose brother **Cathal Crobhdearg 'Red-Hand' O'Conor, King of Connaught** (1201–24) was maternal grandfather of **Brian O'Neill, last native High-King of Ireland** (1258–60), known as **Brian Catha an Duin** or 'of the Battle of Down', who formed a great Irish confederacy but was slain by the mail-clad English in the decisive battle of Downpatrick, and his head sent to London.

By this time, the great Norman-Irish families were well established, and soon became very Irish themselves. Apart from the mighty family of **du Bourg** (usually miswritten 'de Burgh'), **Earls of Ulster**, from whose heiress HRH descends, the two principal and rival houses were the **Geraldines** and the **Butlers**. HRH's Geraldine forefathers include the Desmond line down to **James, 11th Earl of Desmond** (died 1529) and the 'monkey' line down to **Gerald FitzGerald, 11th Earl of Kildare** (died 1585), 'the Wizard Earl', who spent much of his brilliant career in exile as a Catholic after his elder half-brother, the 10th Earl, had been decoyed to London under safe conduct and there hanged, drawn and quartered with his five uncles; while HRH's Butler ancestry from the **hereditary Chief Butlers of Ireland** culminated in **James Butler, 1st Duke of Ormonde**, KG, **Lord Lieutenant of Ireland** (died 1688), known as 'the great duke'.

Since the plantation of Ulster (some years before the *Mayflower* sailed to America), HRH's most important ancestors there have been the **Hamiltons**, down to **James Hamilton, 3rd Duke of Abercorn**, KG, KP, **Governor of Northern Ireland** 1922–45; while in county Mayo there were already settled the **Binghams**, of whom **Field Marshal George Bingham, 3rd Earl of Lucan**, GCB, was the able cavalry commander who saved the Heavy Brigade (after he himself had been wounded) when the incompetence of Captain Nolan had misdirected the Charge of the Light Brigade (commanded by HRH's ancestral uncle Lord Cardigan) in the Crimea.

But of all HRH's Irish ancestors, beside **King Brian 'Boru'**, perhaps the most notable was **'Red Hugh' O'Neill**, called by the Gaels last native **King of Ulster** 1598–1603 and by the English the **2nd Earl of Tyrone** 1585–1608, 'the last and one of the greatest of Gaelic kings', who led the final Irish resistance for years before being forced to submit in 1603, then driven into exile in the 'Flight of the Earls', to die in Rome as **Prince O'Neill**. It must have seemed the end of his line, after more than a thousand years. However, by an irony of history, while his chief foe, the Welsh Queen Elizabeth I of England, died childless, as did Ireland's other great enemy, the Dutchman King William III; it is **Red Hugh O'Neill, last native King of Ulster**'s own direct descendant, **Queen Elizabeth II**, who today sits upon the throne of Northern Ireland.

FERGUS *the Great 'mac Erc', K. of Scots of Dalriada (straddling Irish Channel from Antrim to Argyll), killed 501*

DOMANGART I, *K. of Scots of Dalriada (Argyll or the 'Frontier of the Gael'), d. c.506*

GABHRAN, *K. of Scots of Argyll, killed by his nephew & successor c.559; m.* INGENACH *or* LLEIAN *(niece of K. Cunobelin or Cymbeline), maternal granddau. of* DYFNWAL, *K. of Dunbarton*

AIDAN, *K. of Scots of Argyll, ordained K. by his cousin St Columba c.574, killed c.608*

EOCHAID *Buidhe, K. of Scots of Argyll, perhaps also maternally K. of the Picts, d. c.629*

DOMNALL *Brecc 'the Speckled', K. of Scots of Argyll, slain in battle against Britons at Strathcarron c.643*

DOMANGART II, *K. of Scots of Argyll, killed c.673*

EOCHAID *'Crook-Nose', K. of Scots of Argyll, killed 697*

EOCHAID III, *K. of Scots of Argyll (last also to reign in Irish Dalriada), d.733*

AEDH *Find 'the White', K. of Scots of Argyll, legislator, at war with Picts 768, killed 778*

EOCHAID *'the Venomous', K. of Scots of Argyll, c.780; m. Pictish princess royal, sister of Constantine, K. of Picts 789–820 & Unuist, K. of Picts 820–34*

ALPIN, *K. of Scots of Argyll, killed in battle c.834, probably claiming Pictish throne*

KENNETH *mac Alpin, K. of the Picts & Scots, united both nations through his Pictish royal blood, d.860*

CONSTANTINE I, *K. of the Picts & Scots, with his royal city at Scone, killed in battle against the Norsemen 877*

DOMNALL II, *K. of Alba (united Pictland & Argyll), slain 900, buried on Iona*

MALCOLM I, *K. of Alba (Albany, modern Scotland north of the Forth & Clyde), slain by the Moray men 954*

KENNETH II, *K. of the Scots of Alba, killed on behalf of his Moray cousin & successor 995*

MALCOLM II, *K. of Scots, mortally wounded by rival branches of royal house 1034*

BETHOC, *heiress of the kingdom at Scone, m.* CRINAN, *hereditary Abbot of Dunkeld (of the Kindred of St Columba), killed in battle 1045*

DUNCAN I, *K. of Scots, killed by his cousin & successor Macbeth 1040*

MALCOLM *Ceann-Mor, K. of Scots, slew K. Macbeth 1057, killed invading England 1093*

DAVID I *'the Saint', K. of Scots (son of St* MARGARET, *Anglo-Saxon princess) united Alba, Lothian & Cumbria, d.1153*

HENRY, *King-Designate of Scots, Earl of Northumberland & Huntingdon, predeceased father 1152*

DAVID, *Earl of Huntingdon, d.1219 (bro. of K. Malcolm the Maiden & K.* WILLIAM *the Lyon)*

Lady ISABEL *the Scot, d. c.1251 (sister & heiress of John the Scot, Earl of Chester & Huntingdon); m.* ROBERT *'the Noble' de Bruce, Lord of Annandale, with his chief castle at Lochmaben, d.1245*

ROBERT *de Bruce, Lord of Annandale, nominated heir-presumptive to the Crown 1238, Competitor for the Crown 1292, d.1294*

ROBERT *de Bruce, Earl of Carrick, kidnapped by* MARJORIE, *Countess of Carrick in her own right, whom he married, d.1304*

ROBERT *the Bruce, K. of Scots, crowned at Scone 1306, victor of Bannockburn 1314, Scotland's liberator, d.1329*

MARJORIE *of Scotland, d.1315 (half-sister of David* II
Bruce, K. of Scots 1329–70); m. WALTER,
*6th hereditary Great Steward of Scotland,
d.1326 (whose father* JAMES *the Steward
fought for* HRH's *cousin Wallace)*

ROBERT II *Stewart, K. of Scots, as Great Steward
saved the Scots army after Nevill's Cross
1346, became K. 1370–90*

ROBERT III *Stewart, K. of Scots 1390–1406, reigned
but too delicate to rule (so his bro.* ROBERT,
Duke of Albany was Regent)

JAMES I *Stewart, K. of Scots, captured at sea in truce
& prisoner of English 1406–24, assassinated
1437*

JAMES II *Stewart, K. of Scots, nicknamed 'Fiery Face'
from a birth-mark, accidentally killed by a
cannon 1460*

JAMES III *Stewart, K. of Scots, defeated in a rebellion
led by the* DOUGLASES & HOMES, *slain in
flight 1488*

JAMES IV *Stewart, K. of Scots, killed with the
'Flowers of the Forest' at Flodden 1513*

JAMES V *Stewart, K. of Scots, founded the Court of
Session, d.1542*

MARY, *Queen of Scots, beheaded 1587; m.* HENRY
*Stuart, K. Consort of Scots, formerly styled
Lord Darnley, strangled 1567*

JAMES I, *K. of Great Britain (formerly* JAMES VI, *K.
of Scots) 1603–25*

ancestors of HRH   *See Tables 7 & 8*

PICTS & SCOTS

THE Romans never conquered the Picts of Caledonia 'stern and wild', and since the Queen reigns north of the Forth by virtue of her Pictish royal blood, Her Majesty at Scone is head of the oldest continuing dynasty in Christendom. There have been many succession disputes *within the royal family*, from the battle of Moncreiffe in AD 728 between two of HRH's then relations, Kings Onuist and Elpin, down to that at Culloden a thousand years later between two 25-year-old kinsmen of the same Blood Royal, HRH's ancestral first cousin Bonnie Prince Charlie and HRH's ancestral grand-uncle Cumberland. But these disputes have always been between rival descendants of the original Blood Royal, although of course the throne has often passed in the female line: thus nobody today regards Prince Charles as not belonging to Queen Victoria's royal family, yet her present heir male is the Duke of Gloucester, and both equally share the ancient Pictish Blood Royal.

Indeed, the Pictish throne originally passed *only* in the female line, for a Pict belonged to his mother's family: unless she was a Pict, he wasn't considered a Pict at all. The Pictish royal family was therefore matrilinear, and Pictish kings reigned by virtue of being the sons of Pictish Princesses Royal: kings being succeeded first by their brothers (by the same royal mother) and then by their sister's sons. They also appear to have followed what social anthropologists call the 'classificatory system',

whereby the 'true family' are the descendants of a particular great-grandparent, and the eldest reigns, so that brothers and first cousins succeed each other in order of age before proceeding to the next generation. Foreign kings or princes often fathered future Pictish kings by Pictish Princesses Royal before returning to their own country, whether Gwynedd or Northumbria or Dalriada. A Caledonian princess in the third century AD retorted to the Roman empress Julia: 'We satisfy the necessities of nature in a more commendable manner than you Romans, for whereas you seek secrecy to prostitute yourselves to the vilest of men, we appear in the face of the world enjoying the society of the best.' Thus HRH's ancestor **King Maelgwn of Gwynedd** was father of Bruide, King of the Picts c.555–84, and at least eight other such cases can be cited up to the ninth century.

Pictland was modern Scotland north of the Forth: the ancient Alba, or Albany, with her eventual High-Kings' palace at Forteviot, their inauguration Stone of Destiny (of local Scone sandstone, and now in Westminster Abbey) on an artificial mound still at Scone made of earth brought from all parts of the realm (as in Bohemia), and their sacred place at Abernethy: all within a radius of six miles around the prehistoric dry-stone fortress of Dun Monaid on Moncreiffe Hill, evidently occupied in Pictish times by these 'Kings of Monaid'. Abernethy was dedicated in Christian times to St Bride,

Pictish Princess Royal beneath the sacred emblem of the crescent and V-rod

and was doubtless on the site of a pagan temple to the goddess-spirit Bride, of whom the kings were presumably male manifestations and in pagan times bore the throne-name Bruide in addition to their personal name. Royal sacrifice was evidently by drowning, as befits the ancient connection between water and goddess-spirits: the Pictish king of Atholl was drowned by the Pictish High-King Onuist in 739, and women were executed by drowning in some parts of former Pictland as late as the seventeenth century.

There were originally a number of Pictish local kingdoms, traditionally seven, and the nuclear one which eventually established the high-kingship was that of the Fortrinn, known to the Romans as the Verturiones and occupying Strathearn and southern Gowrie as far as the Isla. As with Munster against Tara in Ireland, Moray seems to have been the local kingdom to hold out longest against Scone.

A separate kingdom was established during the fifth century by Scots from Ireland ('Scot' meant 'Irishman' as late as the eleventh century). They were colonists who crossed the Irish Channel from Antrim, and settled in Argyll, which means the 'Frontier of the Gael'. They belonged to the local Irish kingdom of Dalriada, whose sacral royal kings were traced by the Gaelic sennachies back to the Celtic god-king Eremon. When the Ui Neill pressed northwards from Tara into Ulster in the fifth century, **Fergus Mor mac Erc, King of Dalriada** (slain 501) shifted the centre of his little kingdom from Antrim to Dunadd in Argyll; and by the eighth century the two halves of the kingdom of Dalriada had separated, and Argyll became independent altogether.

In 848–9 there was a vital dispute about the succession to the Pictish throne. One of the claimants, by virtue of his Pictish royal blood in the female line, was **Kenneth mac Alpin, King of the Scots of Argyll**. According to tradition, he solved the problem by literally liquidating his rivals: that is, he got them all drunk at a conference at Scone and then killed the lot – after which his claim to the Pictish throne was undoubtedly the best, and he became **Kenneth, King of the Picts and Scots**. The local kingdom of Argyll was thus amalgamated into the Pictish High-Kingdom, at the old Pictish capital of Scone, but the laws were changed from matrilinear to patrilinear succession except in cases where there was only an heiress. The 'mysterious' Picts then gradually disappear from history, and little survives from their civilisation save some beautiful gold-work in the St Ninian's Isle treasure and their finely carved memorial stones. But there is no real mystery about their disappearance: since a man could only be a Pict on his mother's side, and the great Pictish ladies married Scottish nobles of dynastic stock, nobody was consciously Pictish any more after a few generations. But the later Kings of Scots were ultimately only there because of their Pictish royal blood: there was no racial conquest, only a change of law.

The Gaels, however, also had the 'classificatory' system, though with them the 'true family' (symbolised by a Hand), were the male-line descendants of their great-grandfather. So kings continued to be succeeded by their brothers or cousins in order of age, often alternating between two or even three branches of the dynasty. The next three centuries saw the ancient Gaelic custom whereby the king was traditionally obliged to demonstrate his continuing vigour, as the living casket of his people's good luck, by constant defence against his heir, who had what almost amounted to a duty to try and slay him. In Scotland between 864 and 1230, there is the familiar sequence: e.g. **King Duncan I**, slain 1040 by King Macbeth, slain 1057 by **King Malcolm III**, slain in battle 1093 by the English, succeeded by **King Duncan II**, slain 1094 by **King Donald Ban**, blinded 1097 by his successor King Edgar, son of **St Margaret**. The practice was put a stop to by the descendants of **St Margaret**, who stood together against all comers, slaying rival potential heirs.

St Margaret's youngest son, **King David the Saint** (1124–53), united Albany with Lothian and Cumbria, and also abolished the 'classificatory' system, so that the throne eventually passed according to the system that we would recognise today. During his reign, and that of his immediate successors, the Scottish nobility received by royal invitation an influx of Anglo-Norman, Northumbrian, Flemish and Breton baronial blood: founding among others the great houses that were to become the **Black Douglas earls of Douglas** and the **Red Douglas earls of Angus**, the polished **Lindsay earls of Crawford** and the haughty **Hay earls of Erroll**, lords high constable of Scotland, also the proud **Graham earls of Montrose** and the adventurous **Sinclair earls of Caithness** (who built that Gothic masonic gem, Rosslyn Chapel) from all of which famous families HRH descends.

By the twelfth century, however, the original Pictish local kingdoms, later ruled over by mormaers, had become earldoms in families of the old Celtic dynastic stock. The Seven Earls of Scotland were very grand: among them HRH's ancestors **'Duncan, by the Grace of God Earl of Fife'** (1154–1204), chief of the premier Clan Macduff that had pre-eminent special privileges, **'Gilbert mac Ferteth, by the Indulgence of God Earl of Strathearn'** (1171–1223) whose line, alone among the Counts of Christendom, had the right to appoint their own Bishops (of Dunblane), and **Gillebride, Earl of Angus** (took part in the sack of Warkworth 1174) whose younger son, **Gilbert of Ogilvy**, was HRH's forefather through **James, 1st Lord Ogilvy of Airlie**. But by the thirteenth century, the most powerful family in Scotland was that of **Cummin**: HRH descending from **William Cummin, Earl of Buchan** (died 1233) married to **Marjorie**, Celtic heiress of that ancient earldom, and especially from **John 'the Red Cummin', Lord of Badenoch**, nephew of the deposed King John Balliol and himself a claimant to the Scottish throne, whose unintended slaying in a fit of rage by his rival the future king **Robert the Bruce** in the church at Dumfries in 1306 precipitated the Scottish War of Independence.

Through the **Princess of Wales**, HRH is an ancestral first cousin of Scotland's popular resistance hero, Sir William Wallace, hanged, drawn and quartered by the English during their occupation of Scotland from 1296 onwards. Through both **Prince Charles** and **the Princess**, moreover, HRH

Inauguration of King Alexander III, seated on the Stone of Destiny on the moot hill of Scone in 1249. The royal sennachie, precursor of the Lord Lyon King of Arms, is reciting the royal genealogy in Gaelic back to King Fergus mor mac Erc

has several hundred different lines of descent from **King Robert the Bruce**, the epic hero who liberated Scotland at the decisive battle of Bannockburn in 1314. The great King left daughters by each of his wives, and the present writer is proud that both the **Prince** and **Princess of Wales** descend from **King Robert**'s second daughter **Maud** (by way of **John, Lord of Lorne**, the mighty **MacDougall chief**) through **Sir John Moncreiffe of that Ilk, 8th Laird** (died 1497). But the throne itself eventually passed through **King Robert Bruce**'s eldest daughter **Marjorie** to her son **Robert, 7th hereditary Great Steward of Scotland**, who in 1370 became the first **Stewart** sovereign as **King Robert II**. The **Stewarts** descended from **Alan, hereditary Steward of Dol** in Brittany c.1045, evidently related to the local Breton counts of Dinan, and thus ultimately Ancient Britons in origin.

King Robert the Bruce's most famous companion-in-arms was the **Good Sir James,**

Lord of Douglas, who was slain carrying Bruce's heart on crusade against the Saracens in Spain. By the beginning of the fifteenth century the two most powerful families in Scotland were the **Black Earls of Douglas** and the **Dukes of Albany, Regents of Scotland**. But **Murdac Stewart, 2nd Duke of Albany** was beheaded in 1425 with most of his family, leaving, however, a **Stewart** descendant whose slaughter by **Huntly** in 1592 as the **Bonnie Earl of Moray** is still commemorated in a well-known lament.

The **Black Douglases** were gradually overthrown by the Crown during the fifteenth century, with the assistance of their kinsmen the **Red Douglases**. From Greece to Zululand the sacrifice of a black bull symbolises the death of an enemy chief, and in Scotland the treacherous beheading in 1440 after a banquet in Edinburgh Castle of the 15-year-old William, 6th Earl of Douglas, brother of HRH's ancestress the **Fair Maid of Galloway**, was presaged by the entry of a black bull's head at the feast. Earlier that century, another of HRH's ancestors, **The Mackintosh (Malcolm, 10th chief of Mackintosh, Captain of Clan Chattan)**, forewarned, had slaughtered the Cummins at a feast when they brought in a black bull's head which had been intended to be the signal for a massacre of the Mackintoshes. Through **The Mackintosh**'s wife, HRH also descends from the mighty **Macdonald chiefs of Clanranald**, and more recently HRH descends from the famous **Sorley Buoy McDonnell** of the Glens of Antrim.

During the fifteenth century too, the Crown had difficulty with the main Clan Donald line of HRH's ancestors, the **Macdonald chiefs, Lords of the Isles**, descended from the marriage of **Somerled,**

Death portrait of HRH's ancestor the Bonnie Earl of Moray painted for his mother while she lay dying of burns sustained in the same attack

King of the South Isles (slain 1164) to the Norse princess **Ragnhild**, daughter of **Olaf Morsel, King of Mann & the Isles**, descended from the **Yngling** sea-king **Godfrey, King in Mann & the Hebrides** (killed 989) and probably of the house of *King Olaf Geirstadr-Alf* of Vestfold (810–40) (see section on Scandinavia). The Hebrides had been part of Norway until 1266, when they were ceded to Scotland, but their royal house, the **Clan Donald**, remained semi-independent. In particular **Donald, Lord of the Isles** invaded the mainland in 1411, and fought a great battle at Harlaw against the **Regent Albany**'s general Alexander Stewart, Earl of Mar (natural son of the ferocious **Wolf of Badenoch**), when **Sir James Scrymgeour, Constable of Dundee and Royal Banner-man of Scotland**, was killed (see section on The Ancient World). **Donald Macdonald, Lord of the Isles** (died 1423) was ancestor in the female line of **James Stewart, Lord of the Isles** 1566–7, afterwards **King James I of Great Britain**, since when every heir to the throne has been **Lord of the Isles**: indeed it is the favourite title of HRH's father **Prince Charles**.

After the overthrow of the Black Douglases, the Red Douglases became the most powerful family in fifteenth century Scotland; and in 1488 the then **Red Douglas, Archibald 'Bell-the-Cat', Earl of Angus** led a rebellion in which **King James III** was defeated at Sauchieburn and stabbed to death, after a fall from his grey horse. The next **Earl of Angus** married **Queen Margaret Tudor**, widow of **King James IV** and sister of the English King Henry VIII. Young **King James V** resented the dominance of his stepfather, and when he escaped from him aged 16 he took his revenge on all Douglases, and even had **Janet Douglas, Lady Glamis**, nearly blind from long imprisonment in a dark dungeon, burnt to death on a trumped-up charge of witchcraft.

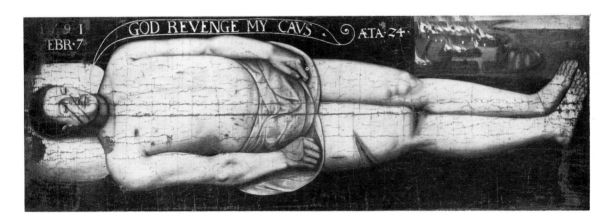

The **Earls of Angus** always claimed precedence before dukes, but during the sixteenth and seventeenth centuries their power came to be eclipsed by the **Hamiltons**, as nearest heirs presumptive to the throne after the immediate Stuart Royal Family, and eventually the **Hamiltons** became premier dukes of Scotland. HRH descends from **James Hamilton, Duc de Châtelherault & Earl of Arran, Regent of Scotland** 1542–44, both through **James, 1st Duke of Hamilton** (beheaded by the English Roundheads for trying to rescue **King Charles I** in 1648) and through **James Hamilton, 3rd Duke of Abercorn** (died 1953). But, owing to the marriage of **Anne, Duchess of Hamilton** in her own right, to **William Douglas, Earl of Selkirk**, afterwards **Duke of Hamilton**, the two families eventually became united in the Douglas Hamiltons.

The **Regent Châtelherault** was succeeded in the Regency by the **Queen Dowager Mary of Guise**, who was ably advised by **Cardinal Beaton** (assassinated at the Reformation), from whose natural daughter HRH descends. There followed the brief reign of tragic **Mary, Queen of Scots**, over when she was only 24, when her natural brother **James Stuart, Earl of Moray** (assassinated 1570) became **Regent**. The next **Regent, Matthew Stuart, Earl of Lennox**, was killed at Stirling in 1571 when his Reformation Parliament was attacked by a force led by the **Earl of Huntly** and **Lord Claud Hamilton**, whose uncle John Hamilton, Archbishop of St Andrews had just been hanged by the Reformers.

The sixteenth century was indeed a turbulent and perplexing time; and HRH's other ancestors then include **Sir James Hamilton of Finnart, the 'Bastard of Arran'**, who murdered the previous **Earl of Lennox** after the earl had surrendered and given up his sword, set 'his mark', a slash across the jaws, on his other prisoners, was the brilliant renaissance architect of Falkland Palace, but was later beheaded after losing a trial by combat and returned as a ghost to haunt **King James V** in his dreams. **William Ruthven, 1st Earl of Gowrie** (beheaded 1584 for plotting to seize Stirling Castle), who kidnapped the boy-king **James VI** in the 'Raid of Ruthven', and whose father **Patrick, 3rd Lord Ruthven**, had been the ringleader of the assassins of Riccio, bursting into **Mary Queen of Scots'** supper room by her husband's private stair, clad in black armour and deathly pale from having risen from a sick-bed for the purpose.

The Border ballads of this time are well represented in HRH's ancestry by **Alexander, 1st Lord**

Coin of HRH's ancestors Mary Queen of Scots with her King consort Henry, wrongly referred to as 'Darnley' by most historians. This coin caused offence by placing his name before hers

Home, and more especially by bloodthirsty **Sir David Home of Wedderburn** (one of 'the Seven Spears of Wedderburn') who slew the French warden of the Marches, and carried his severed head at the saddle-bow; by the bold **Scotts of Buccleuch**; by the **Kers of Cessford** and more especially the **Kerrs of Fernihurst** who bought from the local French mercenaries their English captives so that they could use them for target practice in revenge for atrocities at Fernihurst Castle. The **Kerr** descent comes both through **William Kerr, 4th Marquess of Lothian**, who as **Earl of Ancram** commanded the government cavalry on the left wing at Culloden in 1746, and also through **King James I of Great Britain**'s boyfriend **Robert Carr, Earl of Somerset**, implicated in the Overbury murder.

Turning from the Borders to the Highlands, it had long been government policy to control the West Highlands through the **Earls of Argyll**, chiefs of **Clan Campbell**, and the Eastern Highlands through the **Earls and Marquesses of Huntly**, 'Cocks of the North', chiefs of the gey Gordons ('gey' does not mean gay but ferocious), afterwards **Dukes of Gordon**. In the seventeenth century the squint-eyed **Archibald Campbell, Marquess of Argyll**, leader of the Presbyterians, made himself effective master of all Scotland for a while, but was beheaded in 1661 after Charles II's Restoration. His son **Archibald Campbell, 9th Earl of Argyll**, also beheaded for rebelling against King James VII & II in 1685, was father of **Lady Jean Campbell, Marchioness of Lothian** and sister of the 1st Duke of Argyll. On the Gordon side, HRH descends from the Cocks of the North down to **Alexander, 4th Duke of Gordon** (died 1827), 'one of the handsomest men of his day', through **Georgiana Gordon, Duchess of Bedford**, whose mother **Jane, Duchess of Gordon** raised the Gordon Highlanders with a kiss for each recruit.

Above all, perhaps, the **Princess of Wales** brings

Bonnie Prince Charlie, of whom the present Princess of Wales is one of the nearest living relations

to HRH's ancestry as close a relationship to Bonnie Prince Charlie as it is possible for anyone living to have (since his father has no surviving descendants): that of ancestral first cousin. And she also descends from the sister of Lord George Murray, the brilliant Gaelic-speaking Jacobite general of the 1745 Rising: **Lady Susan Murray, Countess of Aberdeen**, daughter of **John, 1st Duke of Atholl**, who had mobilised 4,000 Athollmen in arms in 1706 to oppose the proposed Treaty of Union with England.

In recent times, HRH has much able Aberdeenshire blood through the **Princess of Wales's** musical Scottish grandmother, **Ruth Gill, Lady Fermoy**, daughter of **Colonel William Gill**, CB (died 1964), and Lady-in-Waiting to **Prince Charles's** equally music-loving Scottish grandmother **Queen Elizabeth the Queen Mother**, daughter of **Claude Bowes Lyon, 14th Earl of Strathmore & Kinghorne** (died 1944), descendant of the marriage of the first **Stewart king of Scots'** daughter to the **Thane of Glamis.**

ALFRED *the Great, K. of the English (of Anglo-Saxon line of Woden-born Scylding kings of Wessex) d.899*

EDWARD *'the Elder', K. of the English, defeated Danes, 'bretwalda' or king of kings of all Britain, d.925*

EDMUND I *'Deed-Doer', K. of the English, energetic ruler, stabbed to death by exiled robber 946*

EDGAR, *K. of the English, reorganised Fleet, said to have been rowed on the Dee near Chester by 6 kings, d.975*

ÆTHELRED II *'the Unredy' (Un-counselled), K. of the English, unsuccessfully massacred Danes & had to pay Dane-geld, d.1016*

EDMUND *'Ironside', K. of the English, struggled to hold southern England against HRH's ancestral uncle K. Canute, d.1016*

EDWARD *'the Exile', Anglo-Saxon prince (nephew of St Edward the Confessor), lived in exile in Hungary, d.1057*

St. MARGARET, *Anglo-Saxon princess (sister of Edgar Ætheling, rightful Anglo-Saxon royal heir) d.1093; m.* MALCOLM *Ceann-mor, K. of Scots, killed invading Norman England 1093*

MAUD, *Queen of England (of 'Kindred of St Edward'), d.1118; m.* HENRY I, *K. of England 1100–35, son of* WILLIAM *the Conqueror, K. of England 1066–87, of Frey-born dukes of Normandy*

Empress MAUD, *Lady of the English, 'Queen Matilda', d.1164, long at war with her cousin* STEPHEN, *K. of England 1135–54; m.* GEOFFREY *'Plantagenet', Count of Anjou & Duke of Normandy, son of* FULK, *crusader K. of Jerusalem*

HENRY II, *K. of England, stern upholder of justice, 'gained in popularity with every year of his reign', regretted Becket's slaying, d.1189*

CONTINUED OVERLEAF

Jewel of Alfred the Great: probably handle for a pointer to follow lines in a text

JOHN *'Lackland', K. of England, obliged to seal Magna Carta, d.1216 (bro. of crusader K. Richard Coeur-de-Lion)*

HENRY III, *K. of England, captured by baronial party under* SIMON *de Montfort, restored by his own son, d.1272*

EDWARD I, *K. of England, established parliamentary constitution in Model Parliament 1295, conquered Wales & Scotland, d.1307*

EDWARD II, *K. of England, deposed by his wife & her lover, murdered by a red hot poker inserted through a funnel in his behind 1327*

EDWARD III, *K. of England, victor of Crécy, started Hundred Years War with France, founded Order of Garter, d.1377*

LIONEL, *Duke of Clarence, Earl of Ulster & Ld. of Connaught, Ld. Lieut. of Ireland, held Parliament at Kilkenny, d.1368*

PHILIPPE, *Countess of Ulster in her own right, d.1378 (Chaucer was a page in her father's household); m.* EDMUND, *Earl of the Welsh March, Ld. Lieut. of Ireland, d. of a chill in Munster 1381*

ROGER, *Earl of March, Ld. Lieut. of Ireland, despite English laws wore Irish costume, but was slain in battle at Kells 1398*

Lady ANNE *Mortimer, Countess of Cambridge, d.1411 (sister of Edmund, last Earl of March, Heir Presumptive of England, d. prisoner 1425); m.* RICHARD, *Earl of Cambridge, accused of a plot against K. Henry V & beheaded 1415*

RICHARD, *Duke of York, Regent of France, Ld. Lieut. of Ireland, then Protector of England, killed in battle 1460*

EDWARD IV, *K. of England, Yorkist victor during his lifetime in Wars of the Roses, d.1483 (bro. of K. Richard III)*

ELIZABETH *of York, Queen of England, Plantagenet heiress, d.1503 (sister of boys K. Edward V & York, smothered in Tower); m.* HENRY VII *Tudor, K. of England, Lancastrian victor at Bosworth 1485 (great-grandnephew of K.* HENRY IV*) d.1509*

MARGARET *of England, d.1541 (sister of Henry VIII, K. of England, & aunt of Queen Elizabeth I); m.* JAMES IV *Stewart, K. of Scots, killed at battle of Flodden 1513*

JAMES V, *K. of Scots, built royal-tennis court at Falkland about same time as his uncle Henry VIII's at Hampton Court, d.1542*

MARY, *Queen of Scots, beheaded 1587; m.* HENRY *Stuart, King Consort of Scots, strangled 1587 (great-grandson of* HENRY VII, *K. of England)*

JAMES I, *K. of England, first Monarch of Great Britain, united British Isles 1603, d.1625*

ancestors of HRH   *See Tables 7 & 8*

HUGH, *lord le Despencer, Justiciar of England, sat in Montfort's Parliament, slain at Evesham 1265*

HUGH *le Despencer, Earl of Winchester, hanged (aged nearly 90) & after 4 days his body given to the dogs, 1326*

HUGH, *lord le Despencer, powerful boyfriend of K.* EDWARD II; *hanged, drawn & quartered 1326*

ELIZABETH *le Despencer, Lady Berkeley, m.* MAURICE *'the Valiant' 4th Lord Berkeley, severely wounded & captured by French at Poitiers 1356, d. of his wounds 1368*

THOMAS *'the Magnificent', 5th Lord Berkeley,* PC, *Admiral of the South & West, co-Regent in Henry V's absence at Agincourt, d.1417*

ELIZABETH *Berkeley, Countess of Warwick, d.1422; m.* RICHARD, *Earl of Warwick,* KG, *Tutor to boy-king Henry VI, Govr. of France 'in great peril & anxiety' 1437–9, d.1439*

Lady ELIZABETH *Beauchamp, Lady Latimer, m.* GEORGE *Nevill, 1st Lord Latimer, became a lunatic 1451 but with lucid intervals, d.1469*

Sir HENRY *Nevill, slain at battle of Edgecote in Wars of the Roses, 1469*

RICHARD *Nevill, 2nd Lord Latimer, fought at battle of Flodden, d.1530*

JOHN *Nevill, 3rd Lord Latimer, pardoned for taking part in Pilgrimage of Grace 1536, d.1543*

JOHN *Nevill, 4th Lord Latimer, tried unsuccessfully to 'ravish wife of the house where he lay' in London 1557, d.1577*

CATHERINE *Nevill, Countess of Northumberland, heiress of Burton Latimer, d.1596 (buried Westminster Abbey); m.* HENRY *Percy, 8th Earl of Northumberland (descendant of* HARRY *'Hotspur'), shot in bed while prisoner in Tower 1585*

HENRY *Percy, 9th Earl of Northumberland,* KG, *the 'Wizard Earl', kept scientific laboratory while prisoner in Tower, d.1632*

Lady DOROTHY *Percy, Countess of Leicester, d.1650; m. secretly* ROBERT *Sidney, 2nd Earl of Leicester, Amb. to Denmark, Chief Govr. of Ireland, d.1677 (nephew of Sir Philip Sidney)*

Lady DOROTHY *Sidney, Countess of Sunderland, Waller's 'Sacharissa', d.1684 (sister of Whig patriot, Algernon Sidney, beheaded 1683); m.* HENRY *Spencer, 1st Earl of Sunderland & 3rd Ld. Spencer, killed aged 22 as a loyal Cavalier at battle of Newbury 1643*

ROBERT *Spencer, 2nd Earl of Sunderland,* KG, *devious statesman, Sec. of State, induced Wm. III to adopt single party govt., d.1702*

CHARLES *Spencer, 3rd Earl of Sunderland,* KG, *Whig statesman & bibliophile, Chief Minister as First Ld, of the Treasury 1718–21, d.1722; m. Lady* ANNE *Churchill, dau. of celebrated strategist* JOHN *Churchill, 1st Duke of Marlborough, victor of Blenheim*

CONTINUED OVERLEAF

Lady Diana Spencer's ancestor Hugh Lord le Despencer being hanged, drawn and quartered in 1326

Honble. JOHN *Spencer, MP, inherited Althorp &*
Spencer estates, d.1746 (bro. of Charles
Spencer, 3rd Duke of Marlborough, KG)

JOHN, *1st Earl Spencer, d.1783 (father of beautiful &*
much loved Georgiana Spencer, Duchess of
Devonshire)

GEORGE JOHN, *2nd Earl Spencer, KG, First Ld. of the*
Admiralty 1794–1801, 'the most stirring,
most glorious years in our naval history',
d.1834

FREDERICK, *4th Earl Spencer, KG, Ld. Chamberlain,*
d.1857 (his bro., as Visct. Althorp, MP,
Leader of the Liberal Party 1830, declined to
be Premier)

CHARLES ROBERT, *6th Earl Spencer, KG, GCVO, Lord*
Chamberlain, d.1922

ALBERT EDWARD JOHN, *7th Earl Spencer, Ld. Lieut.*
of Northamptonshire, d.1975

EDWARD JOHN. *8th Earl Spencer, Equerry to K.*
GEORGE VI *& Queen* ELIZABETH II, *b.1924*

Lady DIANA *Spencer, Princess of Wales, b.1961*

HRH

LE DESPENCER

SPENCER

ENGLAND

T HE English, as Anglo-Saxons, invaded Britain
from Angel in Slesvig (southern Denmark)
during the fifth century. Genealogies have been
preserved of the royal families of Kent, Wessex
(West Saxons), Essex (East Saxons), East Anglia,
Mercia, Deira and Bernicia. HRH also has the royal
blood of the Jutes who settled in Hampshire,
through **Alfred the Great**'s maternal grandfather,
the Jutish **thegn Oslac**. Whatever the make-up of
their followers, with the sole exception of Essex,
whose kings descended from incarnations of the
Saxon god-spirit Saxnot, all the Anglo-Saxon royal
genealogies were traced back to kings who had
incarnated the storm-spirit Woden (for whom see
the section on Scandinavia): **Scyldings** or Skiöldungs from pagan sacred Lethra on the Danish
island of Sjaelland.

Traces survived the adoption of Christianity by
the Woden-born royal house of Wessex, in the
appearance of Woden's ravens in the angles of the
Cross on some of their coins, and in hanging as the
method of execution in England: sending offenders
against the divine natural law to Woden by the

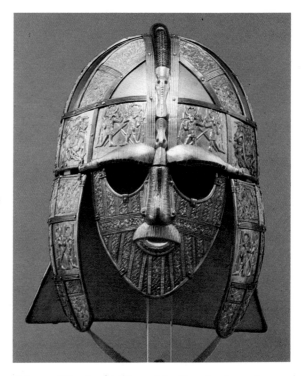

Helmet of Raedwald, King of the East Angles and
Bretwalda of all Britain, died 617, almost certainly HRH's
ancestral uncle

ABOVE William the Conqueror raises his helmet at
Hastings to refute a panic that he has been killed

BELOW HRH's ancestor Harold, King of the English
(second from right), afterwards slain at Hastings 1066

usual channel, as originally the kings who had incarnated Woden were personally sacrificed to their own spirit by being hanged, which gives a fertility erection, and then speared with a sacred spear so that their hallowed blood fertilised the ground. Thus the ravens are still at the Tower because it was originally fortified by a Woden-born king, **Alfred the Great**, and the **Queen** is his continuing descendant.

In trying to disentangle inter-marriage among the various Anglo-Saxon royal houses from the point of view of HRH's ancestry, there seems no doubt that **Ealhmund, King of Kent** (784–6) under Mercian supremacy, had inherited his position by marriage to an heiress of the old *Oiscing* royal house of Kent, descended from the earlier marriage of *Eorconbert, King of Kent* (640–64) to *Queen Sexburh* daughter of *Anna, King of the East Angles*, whose father *Eni*, a *Wuffing* prince, was brother of the Great East Anglian king Raedwald (593–617), thus HRH's ancestral uncle, 'Bretwalda' or King of Kings, who subdued Northumbria and whose magnificent buried ship cenotaph at Sutton Hoo has yielded such splendid treasures. Thus the royal house of Wessex had succeeded by the ninth century to both the kingdoms of Kent and of the East Angles. Through the marriage of the Bretwalda *Æthelberht I, King of Kent* (560–616) to *Bertha*, daughter of *Charibert, King of Paris* (died 567) HRH thus almost certainly has *Merovingian* descents. Again, **Alfred the Great**'s wife **Queen Ealswith**, daughter of **Æthelred Mucel, Ealdorman of the Gaini**, was maternal granddaughter of the ferocious **Ceonwulf, King of Mercia** (796–821), 'the most powerful English king of his time'.

It was, however, under Bretwaldas of the royal House of Wessex that all England was eventually united. This Woden-born family of **Scyldings** descended from **Cerdic, King of the West Saxons** or **Wessex** (died c.534), said to have landed in Wessex in 494 (whose Celtic royal name would seem to indicate inter-marriage already with the Britons) by way of his son **Creoda** (brother of King Cynric c.534–60) and great-grandson **King Ceawlin**, who continued the expansion westwards but 'perished' in some disaster in 593. A more recent ancestor, **Ingild**, was brother of Ine, King of Wessex (688–726), 'a statesman with ideas beyond the grasp of any of his predecessors', who codified the laws and reorganised the Church. From **Ingild** descended **Ealhmund, King of Kent** (784–6), mentioned above, great-grandfather of **Alfred the Great**, who modestly styled himself **King of the West Saxons** (871–901) but may properly be

regarded as first **King of the English**.

However, descendants continued of **Alfred the Great**'s elder brother **King Æthelred I**, victor of the great battle of Ashdown when a Danish king and five of their jarls were slain, who had died in 871 when his son **Ealdorman Æthelhelm** (died 898) had been too young to succeed to the throne. This distinguished branch of the Wessex royal family produced **Æthelweard, Ealdorman of the Western Provinces**, the eminent historian who translated the *Anglo-Saxon Chronicle* into Latin between 975 and 998, **Æthelmaer the Great, Ealdorman of the Western Provinces** (died c.1017), patron of literature and founder of monasteries in Dorset and Oxfordshire, the pirate **Wulfnoth, thegn of Sussex** (brother of Æthelnoth, Archbishop of Canterbury, died 1038), culminating in the great **Godwin, Earl of Wessex** (died 1053), who dominated English history during the reign of HRH's ancestral uncle King Edward the Confessor, and both of **Earl Godwin**'s sons, **Earl Tostig**, killed on the Norwegian side at Stamford Bridge in 1066, and **Harold, King of the English**, killed at the battle of Hastings in 1066. **King Harold**'s daughter by **Edith 'Swan-Neck'** was **Gytha, Grand Princess of Kiev**.

Meanwhile, the line of **Alfred the Great** had ruled England until the death of **King Edmund 'Ironside'** in 1016, when the country was taken over by HRH's ancestral uncle King Canute the Great (1016–35), who was also ruler of Denmark and Norway. At first, the most powerful statesman after the king was **Jarl Thorkell the Tall, Regent of England** during Canute's absences in Denmark between 1019 and 1028, who as a Danish raider earlier had tried in vain to spare the captured Archbishop of Canterbury, St Alphege, offering his companions all he had except his ship in return for the archbishop's life. During the reign of Canute, the rank of earl was introduced to replace that of ealdorman. The mighty **Siward, Earl of Northumbria** (died 1055), known to us from Shakespeare's *Macbeth*, was of the Danish House of the White Bear, a totem from which they claimed descent, but owed his position to his wife **Elflaed**, daughter of **Uchtred, ruler of Northumbria** (murdered 1016), an **Edulfing** of the house who had ruled Bernicia from the Tyne to the Forth since 878. **Earl Siward**'s son, the saintly **Waltheof, Earl of Northumberland**, was beheaded by **William the Conqueror** in 1076, but **Waltheof**'s daughter **Maud** became **Queen of Scots**, and brought Northumberland for a while into the Scottish royal family.

Nor could Canute dispense with another great Anglo-Saxon family: that of **Leofwine, Ealdorman of the Hwicce** in 1016, father of **Leofric, Earl of Mercia** (died 1057), whose wife **Countess Godgifu** was the celebrated **'Lady Godiva'**. The ritual of a naked lady with long hair riding on a white horse had probably survived from the Celtic pagan procession in honour of the goddess-spirit Epona representing 'both the passage of the moon across the night sky and the change from winter to spring'; and the earl's bet was doubtless to dare his countess to take the local girl's place in the procession. Their son was **Ælfgar, Earl of Mercia** (1057–62).

The Norman Conquest took many of the Anglo-Saxon nobles by surprise. The Mercian thegn **Ælfwine, Sheriff of Warwickshire**, had held great estates under King Edward the Confessor, and the family must have made its peace with **King William the Conqueror** after 1066 (the Mercian levies were not ready in time to be at Hastings), as his son **Thurkill of Arden**'s lands fill more than four columns in Domesday Book (1085), and the Arden family still continue today. HRH descends from them through **John Arden**, of Netherdarwine in the fifteenth century, which very probably makes Shakespeare (whose mother was Mary Arden) an ancestral cousin of HRH. But the last Anglo-Saxon thegn to hold out against the Normans was the epic hero **Hereward the Outlaw**, retrospectively called **'the Wake'** after his female-line descendants, the **Lords Wake** (of the great pre-conquest Norman baronial family of **Wac**), whose eventual heir was **King Edward IV** himself.

HRH's forefather **William the Conqueror, King of England**, had previously been **William the Bastard, Duke of Normandy**, so called because he was the result of **Duke Robert the Devil**'s dalliance with the original **Harlot**, daughter of **Fulbert**, a tanner of Falaise. Although he was never keen on actual capital punishment, **William the Bastard** could get touchy about jokes too near the bone, and when he captured the town of Alençon that had displayed flayed skins on its walls in allusion to the tanner's trade, he chopped the right hand and left foot off all the citizens to teach them a smart lesson about laughing last. The Norman dukes descended from **Rolf the Ganger, Jarl of the Northmen or Normans** (died c.932) after whom Rouen was named, and who carved out a duchy for himself in northern France. His father, **Ragnvald the Wise, Jarl of Möre** in Norway, was grandson of **Ivar, Jarl of the Upplanders**, for the

pagan sacral Frey-born **Yngling** ancestry of whose father **King Halfdan the Stingy** see the section on Scandinavia. **William the Conqueror** was accompanied at Hastings by his Yngling cousin **Richard fitz Gilbert**, son of the **Count of Brionne** and founder of the great **House of Clare**, to which **Strongbow**, leader of the Anglo-Norman invasion of Ireland a century later, was to belong.

Other Norman ancestors of HRH include the mighty **William fitz Osbern, Earl of Hereford and Viceroy of England**, who left his mark on the Welsh March before being slain abroad; **Walter Giffard, Earl of Buckingham**, who brought thirty longships to the conquest; and **Roger de Montgomery, Earl Palatine of Shrewsbury**.

Henry I took care to reintroduce the old Anglo-Saxon royal blood into the family by marrying the daughter of **St Margaret**, sister of Edgar the Ætheling, rightful heir of the House of Wessex. But after his death, there was civil war between his own daughter, the **Empress Maud** (widow of the Emperor Henry V and wife of **Geoffrey 'Plantagenet'**), often known by her Latin name as **'Queen Matilda'**, and her cousin, also HRH's ancestor, **King Stephen**. Under **King Henry II** law and order was re-established; so that by the end of the twelfth century **Ranulf de Glanville, Justiciar of England** (died on crusade 1190) wrote his famous treatise on English law; and HRH's ancestral uncle, that great statesman Hubert Walter, Archbishop of Canterbury and Justiciar of England, as effective ruler of England during Richard Coeur-de-Lion's absence abroad, was able to reorganise the whole system of government, introducing election and representation.

HRH descends not only from **King John**, but also from most of the Magna Carta barons, notably their chosen leader, the energetic baron **Robert fitz Walter** (a scion of the House of Clare, and thus an Yngling from saga-time in the direct male line), whom five earls and forty barons nominated as 'Marshal of the Army of God and Holy Church' when they marched on London in 1215, following the king to Runymede.

In the period after **King John**'s death, two of HRH's greatest English ancestors were the chivalrous **William the Marshal, Earl of Pembroke, Guardian of England** and a true knight errant (married to **Lady Isabel de Clare**, daughter of **Richard 'Strongbow', Earl of Pembroke**, 'statesman, as the **Fitzgeralds** were the soldiers, of the Irish conquest'): and the heroic **Marshal**'s successor as **Regent of England, Hubert du Bourg**,

Lirarbus dur Eboraricierundus
filius Edwardi quarti

Edwardus princeps Walli
primus filius Edwardi quarti

Edwardus dei gratia Frebslaue
et francie et dominus hibernie

Earl of Kent, immortalised by Shakespeare for having refused to put out the eyes of the captive prince Arthur of Brittany at the behest of the boy's wicked uncle **King John**. Later in the thirteenth century, the baronial conflict with the Crown came to a head again when their leader, **Simon de Montfort, Earl of Leicester**, captured **King Henry III** himself at the battle of Lewes, and summoned a rigged 'Parliament' in 1265 that nevertheless was the precursor of the future parliamentary system. But the future **King Edward I** defeated and slew **Simon de Montfort** at Evesham, when his head and testicles were rather significantly sent as a trophy to **Maud**, wife of the royal general **Roger de Mortimer, lord of Wigmore**, before being returned for burial in a miraculous tomb.

King Edward I's conquests of Wales and Scotland brought to the fore such eminent soldiers and administrators as **John de Warenne, Earl of Surrey, Lord Lieutenant of Scotland**, who was defeated at Stirling Bridge by HRH's Scottish ancestor **Sir Andrew of Murray** and ancestral first cousin Sir William Wallace; **Humphrey de Bohun, Earl of Hereford and Constable of England** (slain in rebellion against **Edward II** 1322), taken prisoner at Bannockburn and exchanged for **King Robert Bruce's queen**; and the able **Aymer de Valence, Earl of Pembroke** (a **Lusignan** of the House of the serpent-fairy

Melusine), who as **Lord Lieutenant of Scotland** in 1306 was responsible for the initial campaigns against **Robert Bruce**, being ordered by the irate **King Edward I** to 'burn and slay and raise dragon': the terrible dragon banner which meant that no mercy would be shown.

After **King Edward II**'s defeat at Bannockburn, English politics became more concerned with the king's homosexual love-life. The baronial leader was a royal prince **Thomas, Earl of Lancaster**, defeated in 1322 and beheaded, people throwing dirt at him on the way to execution, while his colleagues **John, Lord Mowbray** and **Bartholomew, Lord Badlesmere** were hanged, drawn and quartered. Eventually the **queen, Isabelle** (daughter of **King Philip IV of France**) gathered a party who overthrew the king, who was imprisoned and then horribly murdered. His current favourite's father, the ninety-year-old **Hugh le Despencer, Earl of Winchester**, was hanged for four days, and his body then fed to the dogs; the handsome minion himself, **Hugh, Lord le Despencer** escaped but was captured, made to mount a gallows 50 feet high, then 'hanged, drawn and quartered', which meant being hanged stark naked in public, cut down choking but still alive, having his private parts cut off, being disembowelled and seeing his own entrails burnt in front of him: next his arms and legs were hacked off and

OPPOSITE AND ABOVE
Contemporary portraits of King
Edward IV and Queen Elizabeth
Wydeville with their children, the
little princes smothered in the
Tower and HRH's ancestress
Elizabeth of York, the
Plantagenet heiress

RIGHT   HRH's forefather William
Cecil, Lord Burghley, the leading
Elizabethan statesman

only then was he finally beheaded. This was the standard English doom for treason. That old veteran warrior, **Edmund Fitzalan, Earl of Arundel**, who had held staunchly to the king, was also beheaded in 1326. The **queen** then ran the country with her paramour **Roger Mortimer, Earl of March**, until her son, the young **King Edward III**, surprised their castle in 1327 through a secret passage at midnight, and **Mortimer** in turn was hanged at Tyburn.

Under **King Edward III** and his successors HRH's forefathers included many paladins of the Hundred Years War, among them **John of Gaunt, Duke of Lancaster** and (since Guyenne and much of southern France were loyal to the King of England as their Duc d'Aquitaine) the famous **Captal de Buch** who turned the enemy flank at Poitiers. A French counter-attack on Cornwall in 1339 had already been repulsed by **Hugh de Courtenay, Earl of Devon**. The Black Prince was HRH's ancestral uncle; as also was King Henry V, victor of Agincourt: since although **King Henry IV** has left no lawful descendants, his younger son **Humphrey, Duke of Gloucester**, had a natural daughter **Antigone, Countess of Tancarville**. Indeed, as a direct result of **Prince Charles**'s marriage to **Lady Diana Spencer**, HRH descends from every **Sovereign** or **Protector of England** who has left surviving descendants, with the sole exceptions of Oliver Cromwell (who, curiously enough, was forefather of the present Duchess of Kent) and William IV. During an interval in the French wars, there was the great cavalry raid, that chevauchée or Chevy Chase when 'a dead man won the fight' as **James, 2nd Earl of Douglas** was slain victorious in his moonlight battle at Otterburn against **Harry 'Hotspur', Lord Percy**. The last great English soldier of the Hundred Years War, **John Talbot, Earl of Shrewsbury**, 'our good dog', was killed at the closing battle of Castillon in 1453 when artillery triumphed over armoured chivalry.

To turn to more peaceful things, HRH's ancestral uncle Dick Whittington was Lord Mayor of London not just 'thrice' but four times between 1397 and 1420. For learning and beautiful architecture, too, **Robert Chichele, Lord Mayor of London**, was brother of the celebrated Henry Chichele, Archbishop of Canterbury (1413–43), who founded All Souls College at Oxford, thus making HRH 'founder's kin' there.

Soon came the Wars of the Roses, in which many of HRH's forefathers literally lost their heads: among the last of them being **William, Lord Hastings**, so dramatically dragged from the Council Chamber at the Tower to the block in Shakespeare's play about HRH's ancestral uncle King Richard III. Perhaps the best known of HRH's ancestors to perish in those tricky times (which disturbed the nobles rather than the ordinary people) were **Richard, Duke of York, Protector of England** (slain 1460), father of **King Edward IV**; also **Richard Nevill, Earl of Warwick**, known as **'Warwick the Kingmaker'**, killed in battle 1471; and his royal son-in-law **George, Duke of Clarence, Lord Lieutenant of Ireland** (where drowning was a form of royal sacrifice) drowned in a butt of Malmsey wine. The Yorkists were particularly cross with the Lancastrian Cliffords, as **John, Lord Clifford 'the Butcher'** had avenged his own father by murdering the **Duke of York**'s young son while a prisoner, so when **Lord Clifford** was later slain himself, his little son was smuggled away and brought up as a simple shepherd, watching the stars. When all was safe after **Henry VII**'s Lancastrian victory at Bosworth, the shepherd lad suddenly found himself the powerful **Henry, Lord Clifford**, and as **'the Shepherd Lord'** built himself an observatory. Another ancestor, **Sir Robert Dymoke of Scrivelsby, hereditary King's Champion of England** (1470–1544) must have had a difficult time throwing down his gauntlet in the traditional challenge to all comers at Coronations during the Wars of the Roses.

With the Tudors came peace, and orderly taxation. The taxation was imposed by **Henry VII**'s efficient but unpopular ministers, **Sir Richard Empson** and **Edmund Dudley**, both beheaded in 1510 as a sop to the people. Henry VIII also tended to behead his kin, such as the aged **Margaret, Countess of Salisbury, last of the Plantagenets** who was chased round the block; **Edward Stafford, Duke of Buckingham and Lord High Constable**, whom the emperor called 'the finest buck in Christendom'; and the poet **Henry Howard, Earl of Surrey**, who had quartered the Royal Arms too grandly. After Henry VIII's death, his brother-in-law **Edward Seymour, Duke of Somerset**, became **Protector of England**, until he too was 'brought to the block' in 1552; being succeeded by the unfortunate minister **Edmund Dudley**'s son **John Dudley, Duke of Northumberland**, to be beheaded in turn for making his own son's tragic wife, sweet Lady Jane Grey (HRH's ancestral aunt), Queen of England in 1553 for a few days.

During the Elizabethan Golden Age, HRH's most powerful forefather was the great statesman **William Cecil, Lord Burghley**, who was succeeded as Queen Elizabeth I's chief minister by his son **Robert Cecil, Earl of Salisbury**. Her diplomatic and secret services were organised by **Sir Francis Walsingham**; literature and drama encouraged by her courtiers **Edward de Vere, 17th Earl of Oxford** and **Henry Wriothesley, Earl of Southampton**; science and philosophy studied by the genius Sir Francis Bacon (HRH's ancestral first cousin), to whom some would attribute the works of Shakespeare; the honour of her navy upheld by the gallant death 'at Flores off the Azores' of **Sir Richard Grenville**, fighting to the death in *The Revenge* against 54 Spanish warships; and the Spanish Armada defeated by **Charles, Lord Howard of Effingham**, her **Lord High Admiral**. Other Howards were less lucky: **Thomas Howard, 4th Duke of Norfolk** was beheaded for plotting to free **Mary Queen of Scots**, whom he had hopes of marrying, and his son **St Philip Howard** (canonised in 1970), **Earl of Arundel**, died a Catholic prisoner in the Tower. The Queen's favourite **Robert Devereux, Earl of Essex**, after a disastrous campaign as **Lord Lieutenant of Ireland** against **Red Hugh O'Neill, Earl of Tyrone**, foolishly rebelled in 1601 and got the chopper too, vainly trying to send the Queen a ring she had given him as a safety token.

MARY *Stuart, Queen of Scots, beheaded 1587*

|

JAMES I *Stuart, K. of Great Britain, d.1625*

|

CHARLES I *Stuart, K. of Great Britain, beheaded 1649*

CHARLES II *Stuart, K. of Gt. Britain, d.1685 (& Louise de Kéroualle, Duchess of Portsmouth, d.1734)*

|

CHARLES, *1st Duke of Richmond & Lennox, KG, Duc d'Aubigny in France, (natural son) d.1723*

|

CHARLES, *2nd Duke of Richmond & Lennox, KG, Duc d'Aubigny, Master of the Horse, fought at Dettingen, d.1750*

|

Lord GEORGE HENRY *Lennox, MP, General, Constable of Tower of London, d.1805*

|

CHARLES, *4th Duke of Richmond & Lennox, KG, Duc d'Aubigny, Govr.-Gen. of Canada, d. of rabies from a fox bite 1819*

|

CHARLES, *5th Duke of Richmond & Lennox, KG, Duc d'Aubigny, d.1860, present at battle of Waterloo*

|

Lady CECILIA *Lennox, Countess of Lucan, d.1910 (m. GEORGE, 4th Earl of Lucan, KP, Vice-Admiral of Connaught, d.1914)*

|

Lady ROSALIND *Bingham, Duchess of Abercorn, d.1958 (m. JAMES, 3rd Duke of Abercorn, KG, KP, Govr. of Northern Ireland, d.1953)*

|

Lady CYNTHIA *Hamilton, DCVO, d.1972*

ARABELLA *Churchill (sister of great Duke of Marlborough), d.1714*

HENRIETTA *FitzJames, Lady Waldegrave (natural dau.) d.1730, m.* HENRY, *1st Lord Waldegrave, d. in exile 1689*

|

JAMES, *1st Earl Waldegrave, KG, Ambassador at Paris & Vienna, d.1741*

|

JAMES, *2nd Earl Waldegrave, KG, Prime Minister for 5 days 1757, but defeated by Newcastle's machinations, d.1763*

|

Lady ANNA HORATIA *Waldegrave, d.1801 (m. Lord* HUGH *Seymour, Admiral, grandson of* CHARLES *FitzRoy, 2nd Duke of Grafton, grandson of K.* CHARLES II*)*

|

Sir HORACE BEAUCHAMP *Seymour, MP, Knight Commander of the Hanoverian Order, d.1851*

|

ADELAIDE HORATIA *Seymour, Countess Spencer, d.1877 (m.* FREDERICK, *4th Earl Spencer, KG, Ld. Chamberlain, d.1857)*

|

CHARLES ROBERT, *6th Earl Spencer, KG, PC, GCVO, Ld. Chamberlain to K.* EDWARD VII *& K.* GEORGE V, *d.1922*

|

m. JOHN, *7th Earl Spencer, wounded in First World War, d.1975*

James II *Stuart, K. of Gt. Britain, deposed 1688, d. in exile 1701, m. Queen Mary of Modena, d.1718*

|

James Stuart, the Old Chevalier, 'King over the Water', d.1766

|

Charles Edward Stuart, Young Chevalier, 'Bonnie Prince Charlie', d.1788

JOHN, *8th Earl Spencer (godson of Queen* MARY *& K. Edward VIII), b.1924*

|

Lady DIANA *Spencer, Princess of Wales, b.1961*

|

HRH

Murder of HRH's ancestor King Charles I. Another of HRH's ancestors Sir Hardress Waller, regicide, who signed the death warrant, was reprieved by King Charles II

JAMES I, *K. of Great Britain, 'the wisest fool [i.e. jester] in Christendom', escaped Gunpowder Plot, d.1625*

ELIZABETH *Stuart, the 'Winter Queen of Bohemia', c.1662; m.* FREDERICK, *'Winter King' of Bohemia, Elector Palatine of the Rhine, d.1632*

Electress SOPHIA, *d.1714 (sister of P. Rupert of the Rhine, dashing Cavalier general & inventor); m.* ERNEST AUGUSTUS, *Elector of Hanover, Duke of Brunswick-Lüneburg (in male line of Italian house of Este)*

GEORGE I, *K. of Great Britain, whose Prime Minister Sir* ROBERT *Walpole was also* HRH's *ancestor, d.1727*

GEORGE II, *K. of Great Britain, last British sovereign to command his own army in battle, at Dettingen, d.1760*

FREDERICK, *Prince of Wales, 'Poor Fred, was alive, is dead', kind to Flora Macdonald in 1746, d.1751*

GEORGE III, *K. of Great Britain, driven frantic by porphyria, lost American colonies but gained India & Australia, d.1820*

EDWARD, *Duke of Kent, Field-Marshal, Govr. of Gibraltar, d.1820 (bro. of K. George IV & K. William IV)*

VICTORIA, *Queen of Great Britain, Empress of India, the 'Great White Queen' of the world-wide British Empire, d.1901; m.* ALBERT *of Saxony, Prince Consort, 'a character so pure, & a life so useful & well-directed', d.1861*

EDWARD VII, *K. of Great Britain, Emperor of India, known as 'Edward the Peacemaker', d.1910*

GEORGE V, *K. of Great Britain, Emperor of India, 'a King worthy of his great dominions', d.1936*

GEORGE VI, *K. of Great Britain, last Emperor of India & first Head of the Commonwealth, d.1952*

Queen ELIZABETH II, *Head of the Commonwealth, b.1926; m. Prince* PHILIP, *Duke of Edinburgh, mentioned in despatches at the naval battle off Cape Matapan, b.1921*

Prince CHARLES, *Prince of Wales & Lord of the Isles, b.1948*

HRH

GREAT BRITAIN

KING JAMES I's favourites were of his own sex: he disapproved of sodomy, but seems to have liked to cuddle handsome men. His principal favourite was the talented George Villiers, Duke of Buckingham, HRH's ancestral uncle, whom he nicknamed 'Steenie' and who succeeded an earlier boyfriend **Robert Carr, Earl of Somerset**, whose **countess** had got implicated in the murder of Sir Thomas Overbury. In 1603, one of **James I**'s first acts as **King of England** had been to make the **Princess of Wales**'s direct male line ancestor a Peer of the Realm as **Robert, 1st Lord Spencer**; he being 'reputed to have by him the most money of any person in the kingdom'. His ancestors had been knightly sheep graziers since the time of **Sir**

Robert Spencer, who bought Wormleighton in 1506 and whose son **Sir William Spencer** had acquired Althorp in Henry VIII's reign.

King James I himself suffered from the painful hereditary malady of prophyria, describing his own urine as the colour of Alicante wine, and saying he had inherited it from his mother **Mary Queen of Scots** (I suspect that they, and Henry VI of England, inherited it from **King Charles VI of France**, whose mysterious malady was never diagnosed). This malady descended from him to many royalties, among them HRH's ancestral uncles Frederick the Great and probably King George IV: but the worst sufferer of them all was poor **King George III**, who was driven demented by the unbearable

De Seven Biſſchoppen, werden gevangen na den Tour gebraght.

pain of its mistreatment by the ignorant doctors of his time.

The **Princess of Wales** has brought to the Royal Family descents from the **Stuart Kings Charles I, Charles II** and **James II**. When the Civil War broke out, her direct male line ancestor the 22-year-old **Robert Spencer, 1st Earl of Sunderland**, was killed as a loyal Cavalier at the battle of Newbury in 1643. His wife, **Lady Dorothy Sidney** (niece of the celebrated Sir Philip Sidney) was the 'Sacharissa' of the poet Waller. HRH's ancestral uncle, Prince Rupert of the Rhine, scientist and inventor, was the dashing Wittelsbach cavalry general who later also acted as admiral for **King Charles I**; **James Stanley, 7th Earl of Derby, Sovereign Lord of the Isle of Man**, having surrendered on promise of quarter, was treacherously beheaded by the Roundheads; while the Roundhead colonel **Sir Hardress Waller**, one of the regicides who signed **King Charles I**'s death warrant, was condemned to death at the Restoration but reprieved by lenient **Charles II**, and died in prison. A remarkable character at this period was **'Fiddler' Foley**, the first industrial spy, an ironmaster who acquired the secrets of Swedish steelworks by going round them pretending to be an itinerant violinist.

The Restoration rake, wit and poet **John Wilmot, 2nd Earl of Rochester,** was a contemporary of **King Charles II**, the **'Merry Monarch'**, founder of the Royal Society, and his mistresses **Bar-**

The Seven Bishops, including Jonathan Trelawny, Bishop of Bristol, being taken as prisoners to the Tower of London

bara Villiers, Duchess of Cleveland and **Louise de Kéroualle, Duchess of Portsmouth**, mothers of his natural sons **Henry FitzRoy, Duke of Grafton** and **Charles Lennox, Duke of Richmond** respectively. The five chief ministers at this time were the CABAL, named from their initials, in which the first 'A' represented **Henry Bennet, Earl of Arlington**, whose heiress married young **Grafton**. And by an affair with **Arabella Churchill**, daughter of **Sir Winston Churchill** and sister of the **Duke of Marlborough, King James II** had a natural daughter **Henrietta FitzJames, Lady Waldegrave**, sister of the brilliant exiled soldier James FitzJames, Duke of Berwick and Marshal of France, and half-sister of the Old Chevalier, 'King over the Water', father of Bonnie Prince Charlie.

The **Princess of Wales**'s direct male line ancestor **Robert Spencer, 2nd Earl of Sunderland** was one of **James II**'s principal ministers, and signed the warrant for the imprisonment in the Tower of the 'Seven Bishops', the recalcitrant Anglicans who opposed religious toleration and included **Sir Jonathan Trelawny, Bishop of Bristol**: hero of the famous song, 'And shall Trelawny die? Here's twenty thousand Cornishmen will know the reason why.'

The Great Duke of
Marlborough, whose
daughter Lady Anne
Churchill married
Charles Spencer 3rd Earl
of Sunderland

OPPOSITE   King Charles II,
ancestor of Lady Diana
Spencer, Princess of Wales

HRH's forefather Sir
Robert Walpole, first
Prime Minister of Great
Britain (1715–42)

In the reign of Queen Anne, HRH's ancestral aunt, the greatest figure was the celebrated strategist **John Churchill, 1st Duke of Marlborough**, victor of Blenheim, while another brilliant general was **Charles Mordaunt, 3rd Earl of Peterborough**, the commander-in-chief who drove the French out of Spain; and her Chief Minister was **Robert Harley**, afterwards **Earl of Oxford**.

The eighteenth century saw the accession of the **House of Hanover**, descended from **Elizabeth Stuart, the 'Winter Queen'** of Bohemia, daughter of **King James I**. Under **King George I** and **King George II**, cabinet government evolved, and **Sir Robert Walpole**, afterwards **Earl of Orford**, was Prime Minister from 1721 to 1742; and is reckoned the first premier by historians. This was the century of the nearest common ancestors of **Princes Charles** and the **Princess of Wales: William Cavendish, 3rd Duke of Devonshire** (died 1755) and his **Duchess** (died 1777). **Prince Charles**'s forefathers include the **4th Duke of Devonshire**, Whig Prime Minister 1756–7 and the **3rd Duke of Portland**, also Whig Prime Minister, while the **Princess of Wales**'s ancestor **James, 2nd Earl Waldegrave**, 'perhaps the most intimate friend of **George II**', was Prime Minister for a few days in 1757. English architecture reached its height in those days, exemplified by the connoisseur **Richard Boyle, 3rd Earl of Burlington's** beautiful Palladian villa at Chiswick.

At this period HRH had English ancestors in all walks of life from **King George III** and the great Whig magnates downwards: among them, to quote Sir Anthony Wagner, 'a director of the East India Company, a provincial banker, two daughters of bishops, three clergymen, a Huguenot refugee's daughter, the landlord of the George Inn at Stamford, a London toyman and a London plumber. The story of this last is curious. **George Carpenter** (1713–82) of Redbourn, Hertfordshire, had the plumber in question down from London to repair the roof of his house. With the plumber came his daughter and both remained at Redbourn some time. **Mary Elizabeth Walsh**, the daughter, was eighteen years of age, and **Mr. Carpenter** upwards of sixty, yet notwithstanding the disparity of their ages and positions he married her. Their daughter married the **11th Earl of Strathmore**.' Another surprising ancestor at this time was **Bobby Shafto**, hero of the song. It was also the period of HRH's most adorable ancestral aunt, Lady Georgiana Spencer, Duchess of Devonshire, of whom a workman said that if he were God, he would make her Queen of Heaven.

During the nineteenth century, the British Empire became the greatest the world had seen. **Queen Victoria, Empress of India**, was the last of the **House of Hanover**, and under the influence of **Prince Albert** for good, what was to become the **House of Windsor** set the example for constitutional monarchy: today **Prince Philip** and the **Queen**, as well as the constitutional monarchs of Denmark, Norway, Sweden and Spain are all **Prince Albert**'s descendants. Under the leadership of the great families to which the **Princess of Wales** belongs, parliament was reformed, the slave trade suppressed, and all the ancient horrors of human sacrifice and cannibalism done away with under the 'Pax Britannica' over a great area of the globe.

The creation of the Empire required soldiers and sailors and bankers as well as statesmen. HRH descends from the famous admiral **Richard, Earl Howe**, victor of the Glorious First of June in 1794, popular with his seamen who nicknamed him 'Black Dick'; **Richard, Marquess Wellesley, Governor-General of India and Foreign Secretary**, brother of the 'Iron Duke' of Wellington; **Field-Marshal the Earl of Uxbridge**, who lost his leg commanding the cavalry at Waterloo, giving it a cenotaph there and a ceremonial burial at home; and **Field-Marshal the Earl of Lucan**, who commanded the cavalry in the Crimean War, which a small British professional army won on Russian soil against the greatest military power in the world. HRH also descends from the remarkable City of London clan of **Smiths**, of which Lord Carrington is the present head and who all descend from the Queen Anne banker **Abel Smith**. Another great banking family in HRH's ancestry is that of **Baring, Lord Revelstoke.**

In 1830, HRH's ancestral uncle John Spencer, Viscount Althorp, MP, became Leader of the Liberal Party: 'a leader of unstained character, one to whom party spirit could not attach the suspicion of greed of office'. He declined to become premier, but helped the **Princess of Wales**'s direct ancestor **Charles, 2nd Earl Grey**, who therefore took over as Liberal **Prime Minister**, to pilot through parliament the Great Reform Bill of 1832: the measure that set Britain on the road to democracy. Another of the **Princess of Wales**'s ancestral uncles, Lord John Russell (grandfather of the philosopher Bertrand Russell), the 'stormy petrel' of politics, was also Liberal Prime Minister. Again, from 1902 to 1905 HRH's ancestral uncle John, 5th Earl Spencer, was Liberal leader in the House of Lords, 'and early in 1905, when a change of

The Princess of Wales's ancestor Earl Grey, the Prime
Minister who passed the great Reform Bill

government was seen to be probable, it was
thought in some quarters that he would be the most
suitable Liberal prime minister. But his health
broke down just at this time, and he took no further
part in political life.'

In the third quarter of the twentieth century,
HRH's grandparents are the **Queen, Head of the
Commonwealth; Prince Philip, Duke of
Edinburgh**, whose maternal grandfather **Prince
Louis of Battenberg** (afterwards **Louis Mount-
batten, Marquess of Milford Haven**) was the

resolute **First Sea Lord** who kept the Royal Navy
mobilised and ready at the outbreak of the First
World War, and whose son Louis, Earl Mountbat-
ten of Burma, was Viceroy of India and head of our
Armed Services; **John, 8th Earl Spencer**, former
Chairman of the National Association of Boys'
Clubs; and the **Honble. Frances Ruth Burke
Roche** (now Mrs Shand Kydd), daughter of
Edmund Maurice Roche, 4th Lord Fermoy, a
member of Parliament before becoming a Peer of
the Realm.

Lady Georgiana Spencer, Duchess of Devonshire. The
most famous Spencer lady before the Princess of Wales

HRH's ancestress Queen Victoria
accompanied by HRH's ancestral uncle the
'Iron Duke' of Wellington

Queen Elizabeth II,
Head of the Commonwealth,
by Pietro Annigoni

VOLOGAESES V, *Great K. of Parthia, including Persia & Babylonia, 191–208 AD (of imperial dynasty founded in 249 BC)*

CHOSROES I, *K. of Armenia 191–216 AD, client kingdom of Persian empire*

TIRIDATES II, *K. of Armenia 216–52, maintained pagan Zoroastrian fire-altars*

CHOSROES II *the Valiant, K. of Western Armenia, slain by bros. 287*

Tiran (Helios) TIRIDATES IV, *first Christian K. of Armenia, 298–330 (converted by St* GREGORY)

CHOSROES III, *K. of Armenia 330–9*

BAMBISHN *of Armenia; m.* ATHENOGENES, *son of* HESYCHIUS, *Primate of Armenia 343–8*

St NARSES *the Great, hereditary Bishop & Primate of Armenia 355–73*

St ISAAC *the Great, hereditary Bishop & Primate of Armenia 378–438*

SAHAKANOYSH, *the Gregorid heiress; m.* HAMAZASP I, *Prince of the Mamikonids 387–432*

HAMAZASPIAN, *Mamikonid prince (bro. of St Vardan & St Hamayeak, both killed in battle 451)*

HAMAYEAK, *Mamikonid prince in Armenia, under Persian suzerainty*

MUSHEL, *Mamikonid prince, living 555, under Roman suzerainty*

DAVID, *Mamikonid prince, c.600, under Persian suzerainty*

HAMAZASP II, *Byzantine Curopalates, Prince of the Mamikonids & heir of Gregorid domain, Prince of Armenia 655–8*

HRAHAT, *Mamikonid prince in Armenia, under Arab suzerainty*

DAVID, *Mamikonid prince, d.744 (bro. of Gregory I, Prince of Armenia 748–50)*

SAMUEL II, *Prince of the Mamikonids & heir of Gregorid domain, killed at battle of Bagravandène 772*

Mamikonid princess; m. SMBAT VII, *Prince of the Bagratids, Constable of Armenia for Caliph, killed 772*

ASHOT *the Carnivorous, presiding Prince of Armenia 806–26*

HRIPSIME, *Bagratid princess; m.* HAMAZASP II *Artsruni, Prince of Vaspurakan c.800*

ASHOT-ABULABAS I *Artsruni, Prince of Vaspurakan (round Lake Van, now Turkey) 836–74*

GRIGOR DERENIK *Artsruni, Prince of Vaspurakan 857–68 and 874–86*

KHACH'IK GAGIK II *Artsruni, K. of Vaspurakan (crowned by Caliph Moktadir), d.943*

ABUSAHL HAMAZASP III *Artsruni, K. of Vaspurakan 958–68 (island church of Akhtamar on Lake Van built by his father)*

DERENIK, *Artsrunid prince (bro. of Sennacherib John Artsruni, K. of Vaspurakan 1003–21)*

KHACHI'K *Artsruni, Prince of T'ornavan, nicknamed 'the Deaf', killed in battle 1042*

HASAN, *Artsrunid prince (bro. of Ischkhanik Artsruni, the 'Little Prince' killed in battle 1042)*

ABULGHARIB *Artsruni, Byzantine Governor of Tarsus in Cilicia, after Turkish victory at Manzikert overthrew Armenia 1071*

ARTSRUNID *princess; m.* OSHIN I, *Prince of Lampron, Governor of Western Cilicia, d.1110*

HETUM II, *Prince of Lampron, Byzantine Governor of Tarsus, with rank of Sebastus, d.1143*

OSHIN II, *Prince of Lampron, Sebastus, d.1170, captured in battle 1152 by* THOROS, *Lord of the Mountains*

HETUM III, *Prince of Lampron 1170–1200, retired to a monastery and d. a monk 1218*

|
CONSTANTINE *the Thagadir, Prince of Lampron, 'Prince of Princes', captured by Sultan of Konia but ransomed, d.1249*

|
HETUM IV, *Lord of Lampron, d.1250 (whose Hetumid cousin became* HETUM I, *K. of Armenia in Cilicia 1226–69)*

|
ALICE *of Lampron, m. the Crusader baron* BALIAN *of Ibelin, Seneschal of Cyprus, who d.1302*

|
GUY *of Ibelin, Seneschal of Cyprus, d.1308*

|
ALICE *of Ibelin; married* HUGH IV *de Lusignan, K. of Cyprus 1324–58, titular K. of Jerusalem*

|
JAMES *de Lusignan, K. of Cyprus 1382–98, titular K. of Armenia*

ancestors of HRH   *See Table 14*

Note: the dots indicate probable affiliations. But the ultimate lineage is not in doubt, since (i) Prince Khachi'k the Deaf (slain 1042) belonged as an Artsrunid prince to the royal house of Vaspurakan, and (ii) Prince Samuel II (slain 777), both as Prince of the Mamikonids and as heir of the Gregorid domain, was then heir of the marriage of Hamazasp I, Prince of the Manikonids (died 432) to the Gregorid heiress Sahakanoysh.

Vologaeses V, Great King of Parthia (including Persia and Babylonia) 191–208 AD: HRH's forefather

Hetum I, King of Armenia (1224–68), who rode all the way to Mongolia to pay homage at the court of the Great Khan

THE ANCIENT WORLD

BECAUSE we haven't got records of all the marriages of ancient royal houses, the furthest back HRH's royal ancestry can be traced at present is to **Pharnabazus** or **Pharnavaz I, King of Iberia** in 299 BC, who was born during the lifetime of Alexander the Great (336–323 BC) but threw off the Macedonian yoke. **King Pharnavaz's** capital was at Mtskhet in what is now Georgia in the transcaucasian part of the Soviet Union; and he himself was a prince of the old Georgian sacral royal race traditionally descended from *King Karthlos* (son of *Thargamos*), the founder of Mtskhet.

His descendant, **Pharasmenes III, King of Iberia** 135–185 AD, was father of the princess who married the greatest emperor in the then world: **Arsakes Vologaeses V Dikaios Epiphanes Philhellen, sacral Great King of Parthia** 191–208, whose empire included Persia and Mesopotamia and Babylonia, extending from the Hindu Kush mountains to its client kingdom of Armenia on the Black Sea. Indeed, **Vologaeses V** had been **King of Armenia** before he succeeded to the **Parthian imperial throne**. And if we but knew all the marriages and blood-links of this mighty family and their descendants, we would probably find descents from even further back into the mists of antiquity, from the Achaemenids of Persia or the Ptolemies of Egypt, and back on to such demi-gods as Hercules himself, from whom many Ancient Greek kings claimed descent.

The **Great King Vologaeses V** himself was the 36th monarch of the male line of the mighty Arsacid dynasty, founded in 249 BC – a generation before the first 'universal emperor' of China. He made his younger son **Chosroes I, King of Armenia** in his place on succeeding to the Parthian throne. The family were Zoroastrians, the religion founded by Zarathustra, which included prayer

through the maintenance of the eternal flame on fire-altars, and which is still maintained by Persian exiles called Parsees in India. The royal house were sacral themselves, and closely identified with the fire-cult, and HRH's pagan forefather **King Tiridates IV the Great**, who ascended the throne in 298, was proud to include **Helios** the Sun among his honorific titles.

But at this time Rome was also still pagan, and a fair Christian maiden called Hripsime fled to Armenia to escape rape by the Emperor Diocletian. **King Tiridates** too lusted after her, but Hripsime was unwilling to yield her viginity to a pagan, however grand, and told him so in no uncertain terms. Instead of just raping her like a sensible chap, the irate monarch caused her offending tongue to be torn out and had her pressed to death with stones: as a result of which she is now St Hripsime and her sad end but heavenly triumph is depicted in the fine church that covers her tomb. For her fate roused the ire of a Persian prince of the **House of Suren, St. Gregory the Illuminator**, who was also fed up because **King Tiridates**, instead of listening to his remonstrances, had cast him into a tower or pit filled with snakes for fourteen years. We are told that, as a result, **Tiridates** was turned by a miracle into a crashing boar, which made him repent, and **St Gregory** had to be sent for to restore him from swinehood to humanity. This may of course be allegorical, but **Tiridates** was certainly converted, and Armenia competes with Ethiopia for the honour of having been the first realm to become Christian. This happened in 314, and **St Gregory**'s family became the **hereditary bishops** and **Primates of Armenia**.

Tiridates the Great's wife **Ashken** is of special interest, as she was daughter of the pagan **Ashkhadar, King of the Ossets** or **Alans**. These hardy horsemen, whose race still inhabits Ossetia on the Georgian military highway in the Soviet Union, kept no written records whence we can deduce their literally immemorial royal genealogy, but they were originally the eastern branch in the steppes north of the Caspian of the Sarmatians, whom Herodotus tells us were descended from Scyth warriors married to Amazon women, and therefore allowed their women to take part in war and to enjoy much freedom.

HRH's Parthian-descended princely ancestors were obliged to leave Armenia proper after the

Dark Age Armenian illumination showing HRH's ancestor King Tiridates as a boar being converted to Christianity by another ancestor, St Gregory the Illuminator 314 AD

crushing Byzantine defeat by the invading Seljuk Turks at Manzikert in 1071. But the Byzantine emperors established them in the mountains of Cilicia around Tarsus, where they built strong castles and eventually founded a new kingdom of Armenia under HRH's **Rupenid** and then **Hetumid** forefathers. They were not always on good terms with the Byzantine Greeks, however, and in 1165, for example, the Greeks captured **Stephen** (brother of **Thoros II, Lord of the Mountains**) and boiled him alive.

Eventually, these kings of the new Armenia had to accept for a while the nominal suzerainty of the Sultans of Konia; and **Hetum I, King of Armenia** in Cilicia 1226–71, struck bilingual coins with the Sultan's name in Arabic script on one side and on the other side his own figure on horseback, crowned and sceptred, beside a Cross with his name in Armenian lettering. This forefather of HRH had a difficult reign, conducted with wisdom. When his real foe but nominal suzerain the Sultan of Konia was routed by the Mongols in 1243, and the sultan's wife and daughter fled for refuge to **King Hetum**, he was obliged, when summoned to do so by the victorious Mongols, to hand them over. Indeed, he not only submitted to the Mongols himself, but, on the accession of a new Great Khan in 1253, 'Hetoum set out in person to Karakorum, then the center of the most powerful realm the world had ever known, and was received with great honors by the Khan. **Hetoum** obtained concessions for the Christians and his kingdom', and returned to Cilicia after a journey on horseback that had taken three years.

A fascinating sidelight on this long continuity of royal blood and custom is thrown by that golden flame: the Oriflamme. The ancient Indo-European peoples from the Baltic Lithuanians to the Vedic Hindus understood well the symbolic ritual whereby fire links earth to sky, as lightning links sky to earth. The sacrificial fire was the messenger between living sacral kings and the ultimate god-head, just as the inner fire of their incarnate spirit shone forth in what is defined as Majesty. So the sacred fire was lit at their inauguration (I myself have seen this done in Buganda) and tended day and night until their death. The ancient Persian or Parthian king-of-kings, the Great King, had just such a sacred royal fire – and when he went to war he took with him a field-chapel in which was the Sacred Fire, to which His Majesty used to offer sacrifice. Over the centuries, the Parthian real sacred fire of their Armenian royal descendants was replaced by a red banner charged with a white flame: the Liparitid Constables of Armenia who often commanded their armies having a white banner with a red flame.

So the crusading Franks from France and Germany who came into contact with the **Kings of Armenia** in Cilicia at the dawn of heraldry met the Sacred Flame in the form of a battle-banner: the Oriflamme. Then red and gold were regarded as the same colour, the colour of fire, and so the Princes of the Holy Roman Empire showed forth their regality with a red banner (later often incorporated in their heraldic quarterings), while the Golden Flame or Oriflamme *par excellence* was the consecrated scarlet battle-banner of the abbey of St Denis, carried on behalf of the Kings of France until the last 'porte-oriflamme' was slain at Agincourt. In 1383, HRH's own ancestor **Guy VI, Sire de La Trémoïlle**, had the great honour to be 'porte-oriflamme' in battle for **Charles VI**.

The Sacred Fire has survived to our times in Scottish heraldry as it is still the heraldic badge of the Scrymgeour earls of Dundee, who have been Hereditary Royal Banner Bearers of Scotland since the 1200s, when HRH's gallant forefather **Sir Alexander the Skirmisher or Scrymgeour, Constable of Dundee**, carried the royal lyon rampant banner in the armies of both Wallace and **Bruce** until captured and hanged by the English in 1306. As 'a Flaming Fire', this badge appears on the seals of **Sir James** (slain at Harlaw 1411) and his son **Sir John Scrymgeour, Constable of Dundee & Hereditary Royal Banner Bearer of Scotland** 1411–60, whose daughter **Elisabeth** married **John, 3rd Lord Glamis** and was ancestress of HRH through **Queen Elizabeth the Queen Mother**. Thus has the Sacred Fire, as well as the Blood Royal of the Ancient World, come down to the present day.

THE BALKANS in the fourteenth century, when HRH's forefathers reigned there

JOHN-ASEN I, *Tsar of the Bulgars 1186–96 with Trnovo as his capital*

JOHN-ASEN II, *Tsar of the Bulgars 1218–41, 'greatest of all Bulgarian rulers' in Bulgarian Golden Age*

HELENA *of Bulgaria, Empress, d.1226; m.* THEODORE II *Lascaris, Byzantine Emperor at Nicaea, brilliant soldier, recovered Thrace, d. in Asia 1258*

EUDOXIA *Lascaris, Countess of Tende (whose sister Irene married Constantine, Tsar of the Bulgars 1258–77); m.* WILLIAM PETER I, *Count of Tende & Ventimiglia*

JOHN *Lascaris, Count of Tende & Ventimiglia*

forefather of (five intervening generations: WILLIAM PETER II, III & IV, ANTHONY & HONORÉ *Lascaris, Counts of Tende)*

JOHN ANTHONY *Lascaris, Sovereign Count of Tende, Count of Ventimiglia, d.1509*

ANNE *Lascaris, Marquise de Marro, Sovereign Countess of Tende, heiress of Menton & Villeneuve, m.* RENÉ *of Savoy, Count of Villars, slain at the battle of Pavia 1525*

MADELEINE *of Savoy, Duchess of Montmorency, d.1586*

ancestors of HRH   *See Table 14*

LYUBOMIR, *lord of Raška (modern Novi-Bazar) 1083, proclaimed Grand Župan c.1100*

UROŠ I *Biyela, Grand Župan of Raška 1113–40, lord of Dalmatia (hostage in Constantinople for his father 1094)*

DEŠA *Techomil, Grand Župan of Raška 1162–5, lord of Dioklea (now Montenegro), deported by Byzantine emperor*

STEPHEN *Nemanya, Sovereign Duke of Serbia 1185–95, previously its Grand Župan, abdicated & d. monk at Mount Athos 1200*

STEPHEN I *Techomil, K. of Serbia 1217–24, surnamed Prvovenčani ('the First Crowned'), d. a monk 1228, m.* ANNA, *dau. of* RANIERO *Dandolo, son of the famous* ENRICO *Dandolo, Doge of Venice 1193–1205*

UROŠ I STEPHEN, *K. of Serbia 1243–76, named* DRAGOSLAV *at birth, abdicated, and d. a monk 1277*

DRAGUTIN, *King of Serbia 1276–82, deposed & became Duke of Mačva, d. 1317 (bro. of K.* MILUTIN, *grandfather of Tsar* DUŠAN)

ELISABETH *Nemanya of Serbia, m.* STEPHEN II *Kotroman, Ban of Bosnia 1272–98, d.1313 (deposed by* PAUL *Subić, Ban 1298–1312)*

VLADISLAV *Kotromanić (bro. of Stephen III, Ban of Bosnia, 1314–53, Bogomil, 'last & greatest of the Bosnian bans'); m.* HELENA, *dau. of* GEORGE II, *Count of Dalmatia, son of* PAUL I *Subić, Ban of Croatia 1292, of Bosnia 1298*

CATHERINE, *heiress of Bosnia (sister of Stephen Tvrtko, K. of Bosnia 1376–91); m.* HERMANN I, *Count of Cilly, Ban of Croatia, Dalmatia & Slavonia 1406–8 & 1422–5*

BARBARA *of Cilly, Empress, d.1451; m. the Emperor* SIGISMUND, *K. of Hungary & Bohemia, d.1437*

ELISABETH *of Luxembourg, Queen of Hungary & Bohemia, d.1442*

ancestors of HRH   *See Table 15*

LAZAR, *Tsar of the Serbs, slain in fatal battle of Kossovo, when the enemy sultan was also slain, 1389; m.* MILICZA, *dau. of Despot* IOVAN *Uglyeša, slain 1371 (bro. of Vukašin, K. of Macedonia, epic hero Pr. Marko's father)*

Princess MARIA *Greblyanova, d.1425; m.* VUK *Branković, Despot of Priština, d.1412 (son of Despot* BRANKO *Iekpal, poisoned by Sultan Bayazeth 1398)*

GEORGE *Branković, Despot of Serbia & Lord of Albania, issued own coins, killed in duel aged 90 in 1456*

Prince STEPHEN *Branković, blinded as hostage at Sultan Murad's Court 1437, honorary Despot of exiled Serbs in Hungary 1461, d. Italy 1477; m.* ANGELINA *Arianiti, sister of Andronica Arianiti who married the famous Scanderberg, 'Dragon of Albania'*

Prince JOHN *Branković, acclaimed their Despot by the Serbian refugees in Hungary at the Assembly of Kupnik 1489, d.1503; m.* HELENA, *dau. of* STEPHEN *Jaksić slain at second battle of Kossovo 1489*

Princess MARY *Brankova of Serbia; m.* FERDINAND *Frangepán, Count of Veglia on the Adriatic*

Countess CATHERINE *Frangepán (Frankopán) of Veglia m.* NICHOLAS, *Count Zrinyi (Zrinski in Serbo-Croat), Ban of Croatia, the 'Hero of Szigetvár', charged to death against Turks 1566*

Countess CATHERINE *Zrinyi, d.1585 (of the great Croat house of Subić); m.* FRANCIS *Thurzó, Bishop of Nyitra, became a Protestant & Comes of Nyitra, Grand Treasurer of Hungary, d. of snake-bite 1574*

ANNA *Thurzó de Bethlenfalva, d.1599; m.* GEORGE *Perényi de Nagy-Ida, d.1597*

GEORGE, *Baron Perényi de Perény, d.1630*

IMRE, *Baron Perényi de Perény, d. after 1650*

Baroness CATHERINE *Perényi de Perény, d.1693; m.* SIMON *Kemény, son of* JOHN *Kemény, Prince of Transylvania 1661–2*

SIMON, *Baron Kemény de Magyar-Gyerö-Monostor, living 1704*

Baroness CHRISTINE *Kemény de Magyar-Gyerö-Monostor; m. 1736,* BALTHAZAR, *Baron Bánffy de Losoncz*

Baroness THERESA *Bánffy de Losoncz, d.1807; m.* MIHALY, *Count Rhédey de Kis-Rhéde, d.1791*

LÁSZLÓ, *Count Rhédey de Kis-Rhéde, d.1805*

Countess CLAUDINE *Rhédey, created Countess v. Hohenstein in her own right, d. after fall from horse 1841; m. Duke* ALEXANDER *of Württemberg, d.1885 (half-brother of Frederick I, K. of Württemberg)*

FRANCIS, *Duke of Teck,* GCB, *d.1900*

Princess MARY *of Teck, Queen Consort of Great Britain, d.1953; m.* GEORGE V, *K. of Great Britain & Ireland, Emperor of India, d.1936*

GEORGE VI, *K. of Great Britain & Ireland, last Emperor of India, d.1952*

ancestors of HRH   *See Table 8*

THE BALKANS

BOSNIA & CROATIA

HRH's ancestor **Stephen II Kotrman, Ban of Bosnia** 1272–1298, was a devout Bogomil. The Bogomil sect of Christianity believed in God rather than the Trinity, regarded Our Lord as Son of God not through divine birth but only through grace like other prophets, and considered baptism only suitable to be practised on consenting adults. They were therefore later on more easily converted to Islam than more orthodox Christians after the eventual Turkish conquest.

Before this disaster, however, the **Ban Stephen Kotrman**'s grandson was Stephen Tvrtko, King of Bosnia, under whose wise guidance Bosnia became the principal power in the western Balkans, and whose sister **Catherine** was HRH's ancestress. His mother **Helena, Regent of Bosnia** during his thirteen years' minority from 1353, was an able Croat princess of the House of **Subić**, whose father **George II, Count of Dalmatia**, was son of the vigorous **Paul I Subić, Count of Split** (Spalato), himself a former **Ban of Bosnia**. From **Count George II**'s brother **Count Paul II** descended the famous **Nicholas, Count Zrinski** (called **Zrinyi** by the Magyars), for whose heroic death fighting the Turks in 1566 as **Ban of Croatia** see the article on Hungary. These Counts of Zrin were thus Croat dynasts of the house of Subić: but the great **Count Zrinski** himself had married a lady of Serb royal blood.

BULGARIA

THE Bulgars were a Turanian race from Central Asia, akin to the Huns and Mongols, who eventually founded what is now Bulgaria. They were originally 'a horde of wild horsemen, fierce and barbarous, practising polygamy', who had been led into the Balkans by their royal *khans* and noble *bolyars* from their previous abode in Great Bolgary (the name reminds us of what used to be called 'the Bulgarian vice') on the Volga. They were at constant war with the Byzantine emperors from their first arrival in Europe, and after the overthrow of the Shishmanovtzi dynasty of Bulgarian tsars, they were subject to Byzantium from 1018 to 1186.

Since HRH's Bulgarian ancestors claimed descent from the Shishmanovtzi, it may be salutary to relate how they were subdued by the Byzantines. One dreadful day in 1018 the Bulgarian tsar saw an almost endless column of 15,000 men in single file staggering towards him, each man holding on to the shoulder of the man in front. It was his army returning after defeat by the Byzantine emperor, who had not slain his prisoners but followed the Byzantine custom of avoiding capital punishment by blinding them instead. Out of consideration for the difficulty of their return journey, he had left one man in every hundred with a single eye to punctuate at regular intervals and thus guide the winding column on its way home.

A century and a half later, HRH's forefather **John Asen**, lord of Trnovo, who claimed descent (perhaps female line) from the Shishmanovtzi tsar of 976, with his brother Peter led a successful rising against the Byzantines, and re-established national independence as **Tsar of the Bulgars** 1186–96. His son, **John Asen II, Tsar of the Bulgars** 1218–41, has been described as 'the greatest of all Bulgarian rulers'. A brilliant soldier-statesman, wise, moderate, generous and just, he held sway over Bulgaria and Thrace, Albania and Greece, including Epirus and Macedonia, and styled himself 'Emperor of the Bulgarians and Romaeans'. His capital at Trnovo was beautified, and in this prosperous Golden Age of Bulgaria, trade, literature and the arts flourished under his firm but beneficent guidance.

For a while, Bulgaria passed under Tatar domination, and Nogai, Khan of the Golden Horde, installed HRH's ancestor **Simleć**, a prince of Cuman origin, as **Tsar of Bulgaria** 1292–1295. However, an independent Bulgarian principality had been rallied together in the country around Vidin by the **Despot Šišman**, whose son Michael became Tsar of the Bulgarians 1323–30, but was slain in battle with the Serbs. Tsar Michael's sister **Keraca** married **Stračimir, Despot of Western Bulgaria**, and their son Iovan-Alexander succeeded as Tsar of the Bulgarians 1331–65, making peace with the Serbs, whose **King Dušan** married Tsar Iovan-Alexander's sister **Helena of Bulgaria**.

SERBIA

THESE Serbo-Croats were a Slavonic race who had conquered Illyria, in what is now Yugoslavia ('Southern Slavia'), as the Byzantine power of the old Roman empire had declined. When they became Christians, the Croats became Catholic as part of the kingdom of Hungary, and were ruled by Bans.

But the Serbs had become Orthodox under Byzantine rule. However, Serbia had been growing up from 1083 under HRH's other forefathers, the **Grand Župans of Raška** (later to become well-known as Novi-Bazar), who were also lords of Dalmatia on the Adriatic coast and of Dioklea (modern Montenegro). In 1185 the **Grand Župan Stephen Nemanya** secured Byzantine recognition of his independence as **Sovereign Duke of Serbia**, and 'was the real founder of the Serb kingdom'. When his task was done, he abdicated in 1195 and retired to become a monk under the name of Simeon at Mount Athos. Earlier, his younger son, Prince Rastko, had secretly left the royal court, became a monk under the name of Sava, then as Archbishop of Serbia founded eight bishoprics, promoted schools and learning, and ended up as St Sava. The saint's elder brother was HRH's ancestor **Stephen I, King of Serbia**, who became known as *Prvovenčani*, the 'First Crowned', when Serbia became a kingdom in 1217. He in turn abdicated in due course in favour of his son **Dragoslav** (who took the throne name of **King Uroš I**) and retired as a monk under the name of Simeon to the Studenitza monastery. It was **King Uroš I of Serbia** who tried to secure an alliance with HRH's other forefather **Charles of Anjou, King of Naples**, to overthrow and partition their joint enemy, the Byzantine empire, but died before it was negotiated.

Undoubtedly the greatest of HRH's **Nemanyić** ancestors was **Uroš IV Stephen the Great**, better known as **Dušan, Emperor of the Serbs and the Greeks** 1346–55, under whom Serbia reached her greatest extent: 'from the Danube to the Gulf of Corinth and from the Adriatic to within a short distance of Adrianople'. **Dušan** means 'Beloved', and **Emperor Stephen Dušan**'s name was invoked by the Serbian troops as recently as their Balkan War with Bulgaria in the late nineteenth century. But five centuries earlier, the growth of Turkish power had brought an end to this dream of empire, and HRH's then forefather **Lazar, King of Serbia**, known to folk-lore as their **Tsar Lazar**, died with the flower of Serb manhood at the fatal battle of Kossovo, the 'field of the blackbirds', in 1389.

Thereafter, Kossovo passed into Serbian folklore, with the usual unfair attributes of blame. **Tsar Lazar**'s son-in-law **Vuk Branković** was vulgarly regarded as the villain, although modern scholars believe he didn't receive the message to bring up the reserves in time. On the other hand, HRH's ancestral cousin, Prince Marko, who has become the Serb epic hero, in real life eventually died fighting for the Turks.

After Kossovo, the flame of Serbian nationality was in fact kept alight by HRH's **Branković** forefathers, until after **George Branković, Despot of Serbia**, a remarkable character, was killed in a duel aged 90 in 1456. But the Serbs had no strong allies, since they 'declared that they would rather be Turkish than Roman Catholic'. They got their wish; although a loyal band of Serb exiles in Hungary adhered to the **Branković** dynasty as their honorary Despots into the next century.

ANDRONICUS *Ducas (Andronikos Doukas), of an ancient Byzantine family*

JOHN *Ducas, with rank of Caesar (bro. of Emperor Constantine XI 1059–67)*

ANDRONICUS *Ducas, d.1077*

IRENE *Ducas, m. Emperor* ALEXIUS I *Comnenus, who regained much of the Byzantine empire d.1118*

THEODORA *Comnena (sister of the good Emperor* JOHN II *Comnenus, 1118–43); m.* CONSTANTINE *Angelus*

ANDRONICUS *Angelus (uncle of Theodore Angelus, Emperor of Thessalonica 1214–30)*

ALEXIUS III *Angelus, Byzantine Emperor, deposed 1203 (blinded his bro., Emperor* ISAAC II*)*

IRENE *Angela (whose sister* ANNA *m. Emperor* THEODORE I *Lascaris); m.* ALEXIUS *Palaeologus, imperial heir with rank of Despot*

THEODORA *Palaeologina, m.* ANDRONICUS *Palaeologus*

MICHAEL VIII *Palaeologus, Byzantine Emperor, reconquered Constantinople in 1261, d.1282*

ANDRONICUS II *Palaeologus, Byzantine Emperor, ancestor of the last Emperors at Constantinople, d.1332*

THEODORE I *Palaeologus, Marquis of Montferrat, d.1338 (whose mother* IOLANTHE *was heiress of Montferrat)*

IOLANTHE *Palaeologina of Montferrat, d.1342; m.* AYMON *the Peaceful, Count of Savoy, 'one of the best princes of his line', d.1343*

AMADEUS VI, *'the Green Count' of Savoy, so called from his green attire at tournaments, d. of the Black Death 1383*

AMADEUS VII, *'the Red Count' of Savoy, who added Nice to his domains, d.1391*

Emperor Alexius I Comnenus (1091–1118)

CONTINUED OVERLEAF

HRH's ancestors Emperor John II Comnenus (1118–43)
and the Empress Eirene on either side of the Virgin

Pope FELIX V *(formerly Duke* AMADEUS VIII), *as
    widower became Pope 1439–49, d. at
    Geneva 1451*

LOUIS, *Duke of Savoy, d.1465, whose wife* ANNE *of
    Lusignan was heiress in her issue of titular
    crowns of Cyprus & Jerusalem*

MARGARET OF SAVOY, *d.1483 (widow of John IV
    Palaeologus, Greek marquis of Montferrat),
    m.* PIERRE II, *Count of St Pol, d.1482 (whose
    father Count* LOUIS *was beheaded as
    Constable of France)*

MARIE *de Luxembourg, Countess of St Pol, Ligny &
    Enghien, heiress of Marle & Soissons,
    d.1546; m.* FRANÇOIS *de Bourbon, Count of
    Vendôme, d.1495*

ANTOINETTE *de Bourbon-Vendôme, d.1583; m.*
    CLAUDE *de Lorraine, Duke of Guise, d.1550
    (bro. of famous John, Cardinal of Lorraine)*

MARY OF GUISE, *Queen Regent of Scotland, d.1560
    (sister of François, 'le grand Guise', shot by a
    Huguenot 1563); m.* JAMES V, *K. of Scots,
    d.1542*

MARY, *Queen of Scots, beheaded 1567*

JAMES I, *K. of Great Britain, d.1625*

    *ancestor (three intervening generations,
    see Table 8)
    of*

GEORGE II, *K. of Great Britain, d.1760*

MARY *of Great Britain d.1772; m.* FREDERICK II,
    Landgrave of Hesse-Cassel, d.1785

Landgrave FREDERICK *of Hesse-Cassel, d.1837*

Landgrave WILLIAM *of Hesse-Cassel, d.1867*

Landgravine LOUISE *of Hesse-Cassel, Queen Consort
    of Denmark, d.1898; m.* CHRISTIAN IX, *K.
    of Denmark, d.1906*

GEORGE I, *K. of the Hellenes (i.e. K. of Greece)
    1863–1913, assassinated*

Prince ANDREW *of Greece, d.1944 (bro. of
    Constantine I, K. of Greece, who d.1922)*

Prince PHILIP *of Greece (now Duke of Edinburgh),
    b.1921*

Prince CHARLES, *Prince of Wales, b.1948*

                    HRH

BYZANTINES & GREECE

Very few people realise how much Byzantine Greek imperial blood flows in the veins of the present Greek royal family. Indeed, when HRH's paternal grandfather the **Duke of Edinburgh** began life as **Prince Philip of Greece**, and earlier, when **Prince Philip**'s own paternal grandfather, born **Prince William of Denmark**, accepted the crown of Greece under the throne name of **King George I of the Hellenes**, there can have been few citizens of Greece who could name any of their own Greek ancestors back to anything like such an early date.

Owing to the loss of records with the fall of Constantinople, HRH's Byzantine ancestry is difficult to trace before **Leo V, Emperor of the East**, who was assassinated in his palace chapel on Christmas Eve in 820. In the case of another forefather, **Emperor Leo VI the Philosopher** (886–912), the difficulty is that although officially the son of Emperor Basil I (867–86), it's almost certain that he was really fathered by *Emperor Michael III the Drunkard* (842–67), grandson of *Emperor Michael II the Stammerer* (820–9). Then there was **Bardas Skleros, anti-Emperor** three times between 976 and his final submission in 989.

The Skleros descent is especially interesting as it brings very grand Arab blood to HRH through the marriage of the anti-Emperor's son **Romanos Skleros** to the sister (possibly the daughter) of Abu Taglib, Emir of Mosul, son of **Nasr ed-Daula, Emir of Mosul** 929–68 (brother of Seif ed-Daula, Emir of Aleppo), son of **Emir Abdallah** (905–29), who was son of **Hamdan, Emir of Mosul** 892–905. This Arab princess's **Skleraina** granddaughter married the Byzantine **Emperor Constantine IX Monomachus** (1042–54), whose daughter brought the Arab blood to HRH's ancestors the Grand Princes of Kiev.

The great Byzantine Greek families who held the imperial throne during the last centuries of Greek rule at Constantinople were the Houses of **Ducas**, **Comnenus**, **Angelus**, **Lascaris** (at Nicaea), **Cantacuzene** and **Palaeologus**, all of them ancestors of HRH many times over through the modern Greek royal family.

Of these, among HRH's direct forebears were **John Comnenus** (brother of the modest Emperor Isaac I, 1057–9, who 'repaired the beggared finances of the empire' before abdicating the purple to become a monk); **Emperor Constantine XI Ducas** 1059–67, in whose time Bari and the last

HRH's great-great-grandfather George I, King of Greece (*right*) assassinated 1913, with his brother the King of Denmark

Roman possessions of the Byzantines in Italy were lost to the Normans led by HRH's forceful other ancestors the famous brothers **Robert Guiscard of Apulia** and **Roger I of Sicily**; princess **Zoe Ducaina**, wife of **Adrian Comnenus** and sister of Emperor Michael VII Parapinaces, 1071–8, who was nicknamed the 'Starver' because the price of corn rose and he was deposed, dying a monk; and the able **Emperor Alexius I Comnenus**, 1081–1118, who had to contend with Normans in Corfu and Thessaly, Petchenegs and Kumans in Thrace, Turks in Asia Minor, Paulician, Manichee and Bogomil heretics, and the Franks of the First Crusade, but managed to regain much of the empire.

Others again among HRH's direct ancestors were the good **Emperor John II Comnenus**, 1118–43, so pure and just in his reign as to be called the 'Byzantine Marcus Aurelius', but accidentally killed during a wild boar hunt on Mount Taurus; **Andronicus Comnenus**, brother of Emperor Manuel I, 1143–80, who recovered part of Italy but had trouble with the Frankish crusaders when the Second Crusade passed through his empire; **Maria Comnena**, wife of **Amaury I, crusader King of Jerusalem**, 1162–73, who was assisted by Emperor Manuel I's Byzantine troops in his campaign against Egypt; the unhappy **Emperor Isaac**

II **Angelus**, 1185–95, deposed and blinded by his brother **Alexius III** (blinding being the Byzantine preference to murdering an emperor), but briefly restored from his dungeon to the throne when Constantinople was threatened by the Fourth Crusade; **Emperor Alexius III Angelus** himself, 1195–1203, deposed when the Frankish and Venetian crusaders besieged Constantinople; his martial son-in-law, the brave **Emperor Theodore I Lascaris**, 1206–22, who gallantly held out at Nicaea after the Latins had seized Constantinople; his modest and highly moral daughter **Irene Lascaris** and her husband, the equally martial **Emperor John III Ducas Vatatzes**, 1222–54, whose administrative ability made the empire at Nicaea 'the strongest and richest principality in the Levant'; their son, the young **Emperor Theodore II Ducas Lascaris**, 1254–8, who reconquered Thrace from the Bulgars; **Eudocia Lascaris**, wife of **William Peter, Count of Ventimiglia** (a pleasant town on the Riviera) and sister of the poor boy Emperor John IV Lascaris, 1258–61, who was dethroned and blinded by his guardian **Michael VIII**, 'and imprisoned in a remote castle, where he died a long time after'; also **Emperor John Cantacuzene** (1347–54), and his son **Emperor Matthew Cantacuzene** (1353–7) whose sister Theodora married the Turkish emir Orchan.

Meanwhile, the Frankish crusaders had made themselves rulers of Constantinople and Greece itself, and HRH's forefathers include such figures as **Pierre de Courtenay, Emperor of Constantinople**, who was captured by the Angelus despot of Epirus on his way to take up his throne in 1217 and was done to death as a prisoner; that stout old veteran **John of Brienne, King of Jerusalem and co-Emperor of Constantinople**, which he defended heroically aged eighty-six in a great siege; the **La Roche** and **Brienne dukes of Athens**, with their residence in the Propylaea of the Acropolis, and their strong castle on the heights above Navplion; and the **Villehardouin princes of Achaia**.

However, in 1261 HRH's Greek forefather, the successful **Emperor Michael VIII Palaeologus**, reconquered Constantinople from the Franks, and the Greek empire was truly Byzantine again. His son, **Emperor Andronicus II Palaeologus** 1282–1328, who abdicated in favour of his warring grandson, was ancestor of the later Palaeologus emperors, who ended with the fall of Constantinople in 1453 to the Turks.

But another of the **Emperor Andronicus II**'s descendants became **King George I of Greece** in 1863, thirty-one years after the Greeks had obtained their independence from Turkey. To mark the occasion, **Queen Victoria** ceded the Ionian Islands back to Greece, and during a reign of nearly fifty years **King George** also recovered Thessaly, Crete and much of Macedonia for his country; before being assassinated in 1913 by a half-crazed fanatic. **King George** was ancestor of HRH in the direct male line.

BALDWIN II, *K. of Jerusalem 1118–31 (closely related to Godfrey de Bouillon of First Crusade in 1097)*

MELISENDE, *Queen of Jerusalem, which Crusader kingdom 'reached its zenith' under her royal father; m. the soldier-statesman* FULK *of Anjou, K. of Jerusalem 1131–43, ancestor of Plantagenets*

AMAURY I *(Amalric) K. of Jerusalem 1162–73 (bro. of K. Baldwin III, 1143–62)*

ISABELLE, *Queen of Jerusalem d.1208 (half-sister of Baldwin IV the Leper, K. of Jerusalem, d.1185); m.* HENRY *of Champagne, K. of Jerusalem, d.1197, supported* HRH's *ancestral uncle Richard Coeur-de-Lion*

ALICE *of Jerusalem, Queen Consort of Cyprus, d.1246; m.* HUGH I, *K. of Cyprus, d.1218 (son of* AMAURY II *de Lusignan, K. of Jerusalem 1197–1205)*

ISABELLE *de Lusignan, d.1264; m.* HENRY *of Antioch, d.1276 (son of* BOHEMUND IV, *Prince of Antioch & Count of Tripoli)*

HUGH III *de Lusignan, K. of Cyprus, crowned K. of Jerusalem at Tyre in the Holy Land 1269, d.1284*

GUY *de Lusignan, Constable of Cyprus (bro. of Henry, last effective K. of Jerusalem until fall of Acre 1291)*

HUGH IV *de Lusignan, K. of Cyprus, so crowned at Nicosia, but crowned at Famagusta as K. of Jerusalem, d.1359*

JAMES I *de Lusignan, K. of Cyprus, titular K. of Armenia, a great hunter, but keen on art & architecture, d.1398*

JANUS *de Lusignan, K. of Cyprus, taken prisoner by Egyptians & forced to pay tribute, d.1432*

ANNE *of Lusignan, d.1462 (sister of John II, K. of Cyprus 1432–58) heiress in her issue; m.* LOUIS, *Duke of Savoy, d.1465 (see also Table 13)*

PHILIP II, *Duke of Savoy, d.1497 (and his beautiful mistress* BONNE *de Romagne)*

RENÉ, *Count of Villars, slain at Pavia 1525 (legitimated as chosen heir by half-bro. Duke Philibert II)*

MADELEINE *of Savoy, Duchess of Montmorency, d.1586; m.* ANNE, *Duc de Montmorency, Constable of France, was at Field of the Cloth of Gold, slain 1567*

JEANNE *de Montmorency, Duchess of Thouars, d.1596; m.* LOUIS *de La Trémoïlle, Duc de Thouars, d.1577 (also descended from* ANNE *de Lusignan above)*

CLAUDE *de La Trémoïlle, Duc de Thouars, Peer of France, d.1604, painted with his squint*

CHARLOTTE *de La Trémoïlle, Countess of Derby, held Lathom House for Cavaliers against Roundheads; m.* JAMES, *7th Earl of Derby,* KG, *Sovereign Lord of the Isle of Man, beheaded by Roundheads 1651*

Lady AMELIA *Stanley, Marchioness of Atholl, d.1703; m. John, 1st Marquis of Atholl,* KT, *a Founder Knight of the Thistle, d.1703*

JOHN, *1st Duke of Atholl,* KT, *Chief of the Murrays, d.1724*

Lady SUSAN *Murray, d.1725 (sister of Lord George Murray, the great Jacobite general in the 1745 Rising); m.* WILLIAM, *2nd Earl of Aberdeen,* KT, *a Representative Peer for Scotland, d.1745*

Lady CATHERINE *Gordon, Duchess of Gordon, d.1779; m. Cosmo, 3rd Duke of Gordon,* KT, *a Representative Peer for Scotland, d.1800*

ALEXANDER, *4th Duke of Gordon,* KT, *Marquess of Huntly & 'Cock of the North', d.1827*

Lady GEORGIANA *Gordon, Duchess of Bedford, d.1853 ('the Bluebells of Scotland' written in honour of her brother); m.* JOHN, *6th Duke of Bedford,* KG, *Ld. Lieut. of Ireland, d.1839*

CONTINUED OVERLEAF

Lady LOUISA *Russell, Duchess of Abercorn*
(half-sister of famous Lord John Russell,
liberal Prime Minister); m. JAMES, *1st Duke*
of Abercorn, KG, *Ld. Lieut. of Ireland,*
d.1885

JAMES, *2nd Duke of Abercorn,* KG, *High Constable of*
Ireland at the Coronation of GEORGE V,
d.1913

JAMES, *3rd Duke of Abercorn,* KG, KP, *Govr. of*
Northern Ireland 1922–45, d.1953

Lady CYNTHIA *Hamilton, Countess Spencer,* DCVO,
d.1972; m. JOHN, *7th Earl Spencer, Ld.*
Lieut. of Northamptonshire, wounded in the
First World War, d.1975

JOHN, *8th Earl Spencer,* MVO, *b.1924*

Lady DIANA *Spencer, Princess of Wales, b.1961; m.*
Prince CHARLES, *Prince of Wales,* KG, KT,
b.1948

HRH

CYPRUS & JERUSALEM

THE Crusaders captured Jerusalem and occupied the Holy Land from the time of the First Crusade in 1097. Jerusalem itself was retaken by the Saracens in 1187 when 'under the horns of Hattin, the hope of the world went down'; but the crusader kingdom of Jerusalem continued, based on Acre, until that in turn fell to the Moslems in 1291, after which the **Lusignan kings of Cyprus** continued to be crowned **kings of Jerusalem** at their Cypriot capital; until the island was handed over in 1489 to the Venetians, from whom it was conquered by the Turks.

The attached table shows but one of very many thousands of HRH's lines of Crusader descent. Indeed, besides the **Kings of Jerusalem** themselves, and the **Counts of Edessa**, the **Princes of Antioch** (founded by the mighty **Prince Bohemund**) and **Counts of Tripoli**, HRH also descends from the energetic rulers of the four great baronies into which the crusader kingdom was divided – the **Counts of Jaffa and Ascalon**, the **Lords of Kerak and Montreal**, the **Princes of Galilee** (with Tiberias for their capital) and the **Lords of Sidon** – as well as from the lords of most, if not all, of the twelve lesser Jerusalem fiefs such as **Caesarea**, **Arsuf**, **Bethsan**, **Hebron** and **Beyrout**, with such famous Crusader surnames as **Ibelin**, **St Omer**, **Gibelet**, **Brienne**, **Ville-hardouin** and **Montbéliard**.

Of these, one of the more notorious was **Renaud de Châtillon, Prince of Antioch and Lord of Montreal**, who avenged himself for seventeen years of captivity at the hands of the Saracens of Aleppo by launching buccaneering against the Moslems on the Red Sea, and by raiding them from his impregnable castle of Kerak or Krak. He broke a truce between the Crusaders and the Saracens by swooping down from his fortress to attack a caravan in which the sister of Saladin was travelling. When he was captured at the battle of Hattin in 1187, Saladin offered him the choice between death and conversion to Islam. He chose death.

It was the Lusignans who carried on the Crusader kingdom to the end of the struggle. And through this romantic **House of Lusignan**, HRH has a poignant ancestral spirit, **Melusine**, the tutelary fairy of their line. She was the spirit of the fountain of Lusignan, a forest spring in Poitou. The tale runs that once upon a time a young lord was wandering in the woods when he came upon a fair maiden by the spring, and proposed to her. She accepted him on condition that he never saw her on a Saturday. They were married in style, and lived happily for a long time, while she bore him an heir and helped him to build the castle of Lusignan from which the family was to take its famous surname. But one Saturday her husband could restrain his curiosity no longer, and peeped at her secretly. To his astonishment, she had become a snake – symbol of water – from the hips downwards: rather like a serpentine mermaid. He rashly gave himself away by exclaiming 'ha, serpent': whereupon Melusine gave a shriek and flew out through a window of the castle, never to be seen again. The date of this unhappy misunderstanding is unknown: it is even possible that an ancestress of the Lusignans had married into a family who in pagan times had incarnated the spirit of the fountain. But the first known member of this distinguished house was HRH's forefather **Hugh the Hunter, sire de Lusignan** in the late ninth century. 'Thenceforth the death of a member of the house of Lusignan was heralded by the cries of the fairy serpent. "Poussez des cris de Melusine" is still a popular saying.'

Fifteenth-century strip cartoon, painted for the King of Cyprus & Jerusalem, showing the story of the legendary Lusignan ancestress: the serpent-fairy Melusine

15 THE CZECHS
Přemyslids · Luxembourg · Habsburg · Jagiellon

BOŘIVOJ, *d. c.894, last pagan Duke of Bohemia, became a Christian (his widow* LUDMILA *massacred by pagans)*

VRATISLAV I, *Duke of Bohemia, d.921 (his pagan widow, Regent* DRAHOMIRA, *massacred Christians including his mother)*

BOLESLAV *the Cruel, Duke of Bohemia, d.967 (murdered his bro., Duke St Wenceslas, 'Good King Wenceslas')*

BOLESLAV II *the Chaste, Duke of Bohemia, d.999, reigned in Bohemia & Moravia & captured Cracow from Poles*

UDALRIC, *Duke of Bohemia 1012–34, at war with elder bros. Dukes Boleslav III & Jaromir*

BŘETISLAV I *the Warrior, Duke of Bohemia & Moravia, d.1055, carried off his bride from convent*

VRATISLAV II, *K. of Bohemia from 1086, as a personal title from the German King, d.1092*

VLADISLAV I, *Duke of Bohemia, d.1125 (his bro. Duke Sobeslav got Bohemia made an imperial Electorate as Arch-Butler)*

VLADISLAV II, *K. of Bohemia from 1158, for whom Bohemia was made a kingdom by Emperor* FREDERICK I

PŘEMYSL-OTTAKAR, *K. of Bohemia 1198–1230, had a long succession struggle after father's abdication in 1173*

WENCESLAS I *the One-Eyed, K. of Bohemia, d.1253, held firm against Mongol invasion of Europe in 1241* ▲

PŘEMSYL-OTTAKAR II, *K. of Bohemia, obtained Austria, but defeated & slain by Germans at the Marchfeld 1278*

WENCESLAS II, *K. of Bohemia & Poland, d.1305, his 'short reign was a period of great happiness for the country'*

ELISABETH, *Queen of Bohemia, d.1330; m.* JOHN *'the Blind King' of Bohemia, Count of Luxembourg, killed at battle of Crécy 1346*

Emperor CHARLES IV, *K. of Bohemia, d.1378, beautified Prague, founded University*

Emperor SIGISMUND, *K. of Bohemia 1419–37, also K. of Hungary, founded Order of the Dragon to combat Hussites & infidels*

ELISABETH, *Queen of Bohemia, d.1442; m.* ALBERT *of Habsburg, K. of Bohemia 1437–9, also K. of Hungary & K. of the Romans*

ELISABETH *of Austria, Queen of Poland, d.1505; m.* CASIMIR IV, *K. of Poland, 1492*

VLADISLAV IV *Jagiellon, K. of Bohemia & Hungary, d.1516, built tournament hall in Hradčany, at Prague*

ANNE, *Queen of Bohemia & Hungary, d.1547; m. Emperor* FERDINAND I *of Habsburg, K. of Bohemia, d.1564, built the Belvedere at Prague*

Archduchess JOHANNA *of Austria, Grand Duchess of Tuscany, d.1578*

FRANCESCO *de' Medici, Grand Duke of Tuscany, d.1587*

ancestors of HRH   *See Table 23*

GEORGE *of Poděbrad, K. of Bohemia 1457–71,*
Hussite leader, appointed Regent from 1451,
then popular king

SIDONIA *of Bohemia (her mother* KUNIGUNDE *was*
dau. of SMILO, *Lord of Sternberg) d.1510; m.*
ALBERT, *Duke of Saxony, d.1599*

GEORGE, *Duke of Saxony, d.1539*

MAGDALENE *of Saxony, d.1534; m.* JOACHIM II,
Elector of Brandenburg d.1571

JOHN GEORGE, *Elector of Brandenburg, d.1598*

ancestors of HRH   *See Table 19*

Wittelsbach

FREDERICK, *'Winter King' of Bohemia 1619–20,*
Elector Palatine, chosen Czech king but
defeated at the White Mountain

ancestor of HRH   *See Table 8*

THE CZECHS

THE Czechs were pagans until 873, when HRH's then Czech ancestor, **Prince Bořivoj of Bohemia**, was baptised a Christian. His own ancestry was traced back to the legendary **Přemysl**. But there was strong opposition to the new religion for about a century, and his widow **Ludmila** was murdered in a massacre of the Christians organised in 927 by the heathen **Regent Drahomira**, herself widow of their son **Vratislav I, Duke of Bohemia**.

There was trouble again in the next generation, between **Drahomira**'s sons. The elder, Duke Wenceslas, was a devout Christian, afterwards canonised as St Wenceslas: the 'Good King Wenceslas' of the Christmas carol, who was therefore HRH's ancestral uncle. In 935 he was murdered, clinging to the church door, by his brother **Boleslav the Cruel**, then still half pagan, who thus became reigning **Duke of Bohemia**, at the instigation of their mother, the dread **Drahomira**. The monkish chroniclers tell us with satisfaction that **Drahomira** was eventually swallowed up in an earthquake: and her grandson **Duke Boleslav II** became 'the Chaste' or 'the Pious'.

Boleslav the Chaste's son, **Duke Udalric**, 1025–34, was wandering in the woods once upon a time, we are told, when he chanced on a charming peasant-girl washing clothes in a brook. The upshot of the interview was that a son was born to the lovely **Bozena** and **Duke Udalric**, to become in due course **Břetislav the Warrior, Duke of Bohemia** and to restore Czech greatness, adding Moravia and Silesia with much of Polish Galicia to their dominions. **Duke Břetislav the Warrior** was himself a romantic wooer, raiding the nunnery at Schweinfurt to carry off as his bride the beautiful **Judith**, daughter of **Count Henry of Schweinfurt**, cutting through the bar of the convent door with his sword.

In 1086, the King of the Romans, in his role as Emperor-elect, conferred the personal title of **King** for life on **Vratislav II**, whose son Duke Sobeslav managed to get Bohemia recognised as an Electorate: with the titular office of Imperial Arch-Butler or Arch-Cupbearer, which entitled future sovereigns of Bohemia to vote in the election of successive Holy Roman Emperors – and in 1158, HRH's other ancestor, the **Emperor Frederick Barbarossa**, made Bohemia into a kingdom in return for loyal support in his Italian campaign by **Vladislav II**.

King Přemsyl-Ottokar II was one of the greatest of Czech kings, acquiring the Austrian duchies and Styria, together with Carinthia, Istria and part of northern Italy – reigning from the Giant Mountains in Bohemia to the Adriatic. In 1226 he routed **Bela IV, King of Hungary** in the great battle of Kressenbrunn. But he was eventually made to give

Elizabeth Stuart, 'Winter Queen' of Bohemia (1596–1662). Ancestress of both Prince Charles and the Princess of Wales

up his German lands to the **German King Rudolf of Habsburg** and, when he invaded Austria in 1278, was defeated and slain at the decisive battle of the Marchfeld.

When Wenceslas III, last of the Přemyslids, aged 17 was murdered by unknown assassins in 1306, the throne eventually passed to his sister **Elisabeth**'s husband, **John of Luxembourg, the 'Blind King of Bohemia'**, an adventurous knight-errant who campaigned from Italy to Lithuania, and eventually had himself led blind into battle on his trusty war-horse, surrounded by his Czech lords, to be slain fighting gallantly for his son-in-law **John the Good, King of France** against **King Edward III of England** at the famous battle of Crécy.

Under his son, the **Emperor Charles IV, King of Bohemia** 1346–78, Czech civilisation reached its zenith. Prague became for a while the capital of the whole Holy Roman Empire, and the Emperor did much to beautify it, building the famous Charles IV bridge over the river at Prague (which required, curiously enough, the breaking of many thousand eggs to mix with the mortar) and founding the University there.

But by the time the House of Luxembourg in turn ended with the death of his son, **Emperor Sigismund**, in 1437, the Czechs had fallen into religious confusion. The Catholic priests reserved the consecrated wine at Mass, while the Hussites, especially the Utraquists, insisted on sharing in the communion wine. HRH's Czech ancestors were themselves split on this issue. For example, one of the most powerful of them, **Ulric 'the lame lord' of Rosenberg**, as **Regierer** of the **House of the Rose**, the most important branch of the great Vitkovici clan, and the grandest of the Czech nobles, began life as a decided Utraquist but, shocked by the fanatical excesses of the Taborite extremists who burnt monks alive, protected the Queen Regent in her flight from Prague in 1419, though later he did his best to persuade **King Sigismund** to have them given a fair hearing at the Council of Basel. **Ulric of Rosenberg**'s daughter **Ludmila** married, in 1431, **Boleslav lord of Schwanberg**, and as a result the great castles of Worlik, Rosenberg and Krumau were eventually inherited by HRH's Czech ancestor **John George lord of Schwanberg** (1548–1617).

Rosenberg and Schwanberg mean the 'Rose Mountain' and the 'Swan Mountain', and another of HRH's Czech ancestors with a similarly romantic name was **Smilo lord of Sternberg**: the 'Star Mountain'. His daughter **Kunigunde of Stern-**

Indoor tournament hall in the Hradčany at Prague built by King Vladislav IV (1471–1516)

berg married one of the greatest and perhaps the most popular of all HRH's Czech forefathers, **George of Poděbrad, King of Bohemia**. Leader of the Hussites opposed to **Ulric of Rosenberg**, who had now become leader of the Catholic party, he captured Prague, was appointed **Regent**, and in 1458 was unanimously chosen as **King**. Other great Czech families at this time from whom HRH descends are **Pernstein** and **Schlick** (who later had a famous ghost story), **Kolowrat** and **Wartenberg**. Their religious troubles continued for two centuries: the principal Catholic leader in the sixteenth century being HRH's ancestor the **Emperor Ferdinand I** (the 'foreigner from Spain' who became **King of Bohemia and Hungary**, and who founded the Danubian empire of the Habsburgs); and culminated in the decisive battle of the White Mountain in 1620, when the Protestant choice, HRH's other forefather **Frederick**, called the **'Winter King' of Bohemia** because he reigned for only one winter, was driven from Prague by the imperialists.

The greatest of the Czech families to survive the wholesale confiscations after the battle of the White Mountain was that of **Lobkowicz**. In 1409 **Nicholas**, afterwards **lord of Lobkowicz**, had seized Charles University at Prague and expelled the German professors. But this powerful family had been divided on the religious issue. The arch-Catholic Baron George Lobkowicz, Grand Chamberlain of Bohemia, had been secretly executed in prison in 1609; while, on the Utraquist side, it was Baron William Lobkowicz who had started the Thirty Years War in 1618 by personally throwing the imperial emissaries out of a very high window of the Hradčany palace: in the famous 'Defenestration of Prague' (luckily they landed unharmed on a dung-heap). Fortunately for this historic family, their cousin **Zdenko Adalbert, Prince Lobkowicz and Grand Chancellor of Bohemia**, who died in 1626, survived because he was leader of the pro-Habsburg party at the critical moment, and HRH descends from him through **Ferdinand Augustus, Prince Lobkowicz** (1655–1715), the grandest Czech nobleman of his day.

The famous bridge at Prague built by Emperor Charles IV (died 1378)

ROBERT *the Strong (Rupert IV), Count of Paris from 822, slain fighting Normans 866*

ROBERT, *K. of France, killed in combat 923 (bro. of Eudes, K. of France 888–98)*

HUGH *the Great, l'Abbé, Duke of the Franks & Count of Paris, subjugated Burgundy, d.956*

HUGH *Capet, K. of France, hereditary Abbot of St Martin & St Denis, d.996*

ROBERT II *the Pious, K. of France, helped by Normans, d.1031*

HENRI I, *K. of France, at war with Normans, d.1060*

PHILIP I, *K. of France, excommunicated for bigamy, d.1108*

LOUIS VI *the Fat, K. of France, soldier-statesman, protector of poor, d.1137*

LOUIS VII *the Young, K. of France, captured Gisors, crusader in Palestine, d.1180*

PHILIP II *Augustus, K. of France, conquered Normandy from England, d.1223*

LOUIS VIII *the Lion, K. of France, led a crusade against Albigenses, d.1226*

St LOUIS IX, *K. of France, 'every inch a king', canonised, d. on crusade at Carthage 1270*

PHILIP III *the Bold, K. of France, supported uncle* CHARLES *of Anjou, K. of Sicily*

CHARLES, *Count of Valois (bro. of* PHILIP IV *the Fair, K. of France)*

PHILIP VI, *K. of France, wounded & defeated at Crécy in Hundred Years War, d.1350*

JOHN *the Good, K. of France, captured by Black Prince at Poitiers, d. an honoured prisoner in England 1364*

CHARLES V *the Wise, K. of France, drove English out of most of France, d.1380*

CHARLES VI *the Well-beloved, K. of France, forced to capitulate to Henry V of England, d.1422*

CHARLES VII *the Victorious, K. of France, supported by Joan of Arc, won Hundred Years War, d.1461*

MADELEINE *of France (sister of wily Louis XI, K. of France 1461–83); m.* GASTON V *de Foix, heir of Navarre, d.1470*

CATHERINE *de Foix, Queen of Navarre, d.1517; m.* JEAN *d'Albret, descended from* CHARLES *d'Albret, killed at Agincourt as Constable of France*

HENRI *d'Albret, K. of Navarre, d.1555; m.* MARGUERITE *of Angoulême (sister of François I, K. of France at Field of Cloth of Gold)*

JEANNE *d'Albret, Queen of Navarre, d.1572; m.* ANTOINE, *Duke of Bourbon & K. of Navarre, heir male presumptive of Capetians*

HENRI IV, *K. of France 1589–1610, Sovereign of Canada, assassinated 1610*

HENRIETTA MARIA *of France, Queen Consort of England (sister of Louis XIII, K. of France 1610–43); m.* CHARLES I, *K. of Great Britain, beheaded 1649*

CHARLES II, *K. of Great Britain, the 'Merry Monarch', d.1685*

ancestors of HRH *See Table 7*

FRANCE

IN the days when the legions still tramped singing behind their imperial eagles down the paved roads that all led to Rome; at the very time when the province of Gaul became Christian with the rest of the Roman empire; one of the mightiest Gallo-Roman families was that of the *Syagrii*, and indeed *Afranius Syagrius* was Consul of Rome in 382. In the following century his descendants, cut off from Rome by barbarian invaders, 'maintained what became in effect a powerful kingdom in the valley of the Seine and central Gaul', and the last of them was described locally as King of the Romans. It has been reasonably suggested that the future **Emperor Charlemagne** descended in the female line from *Afranius Syagrius*'s maternal grandson *Tonantius Ferreolus*, Consul in 453, which would give HRH 'a Gallo-Roman ancestry of the utmost distinction'.

The *Syagrii* were overthrown in 486 by *Clovis* (*Chlodovech*), the Merovingian *King of the Franks*, who gave their name to France. *King Clovis*, who caused his rival Frankish kings to be assassinated (encouraging one to commit parricide and then murdering him) and set up his capital at Paris, was grandson of *Merovech*, sacral Woden-born *King of the Salian Franks* from the northern forests beyond the Rhine; and compiled their famous Salic Law. Although *Merovingian* genealogy is obscured by the Dark Ages, there are a number of likely lines of descent to HRH, very many of the most probable being through the marriage of *Æthelberht, King of Kent*, to the Merovingian princess *Bertha*, daughter of *Charibert I, King of Paris* 511–58, grandson of *Clovis* (see p. 32). *King Clovis*'s wife, the Burgundian princess *Clotilde*, was a Christian, and after praying successfully before a great victory he himself was converted, compelling 3,000 of his Franks to be baptised by ducking in the river at holy Reims.

When the last Merovingian king was deposed by his powerful hereditary mayor of the palace, **Pepin the Short**, he and his young son were forced into separate monasteries and their long hair cut to show that they were no longer royal. The new **King Pepin** was son of the famous **Charles Martel** who had defeated the Arab invaders of France from Spain at the decisive battle of Poitiers in 732, where the expanding tide of Islam was stemmed at last. **King Pepin**'s own son was the mighty **Emperor Charlemagne**, under whom the West Franks of France and the East Franks of Franconia in Germany were united, and Saxony, Bavaria and northern Italy added to their new 'Holy Roman' realm. This greatest of European ruling houses was known as the Carolingians: they divided the actual rule between different branches in France, Germany, Italy and Lorraine (Lotharingia, called after **Charlemagne**'s grandson **King Lothar I**, whose daughter **Irmgard** was kidnapped and married in 846 to **Count Gisilbert**, ancestor in the direct male line of the **Mountbattens**). See Table 18 for HRH's forefathers who were Carolingian Kings of France.

Another remarkable royal family now appeared, direct male-line forefathers of today's King of Spain and Grand Duke of Luxembourg and the present claimants to France and Portugal: while famous branches were to reign in Burgundy, Sicily and Hungary. These were the **Capetians**, from whom HRH has innumerable lines of descent. Their earliest traceable forefathers are **Rupert (Robert), Duke of Hesbaye** in 732, grandson of **Robert (Chrodobert)**, trusty Chancellor of the Merovingian kingdom of Neustria 658–78, son of the West Frankish noble **Lambert**. Soon they became **Counts of Paris** and then **Kings of France**. They take their dynastic name of **Capetians** from **Hugh Capet, King of France** 987–96, so nicknamed, as was his father, because they were also hereditary Abbots of St Martin at Tours: and St Martin had shared his cape with a beggar by cutting it in half, hence the 'Cape' relic.

King Hugh Capet was also lay Abbot of St Denis, and later kings of his line, as Counts of the Vexin from 1076, were vassals of that abbey and thus Gonfaloniers of St Denis, with custody of the sacred oriflamme battle-banner (see p. 52), which was borne into battle on their behalf by the 'noblest and bravest of knights'. A plain scarlet flag with three green silken tassels, the bearer wore it slung round his neck until it was hoisted to hang down crosswise from his lance raised as the signal for battle. In 1383 the oriflamme was borne against the English by **Guy VI, Sire de La Trémoïlle**, forefather of HRH through **Georges, Great Chamberlain of France** (so stout that a would-be assassin's dagger failed to penetrate several inches of fat), **Louis II de La Trémoïlle**, Governor of Burgundy, 'chevalier sans reproche' killed at Pavia in 1525, **Charles, Prince of Talmont**, slain at Marignano, and **Claude de La Trémoïlle, Duc de Thouars** (died 1604), proud to be painted with his squint.

St Louis setting off on crusade (1226–70)

But it was probably with the holy **St Louis, King of France** himself, that the practice of 'touching for the King's Evil' originated, and scruffy sufferers from scrofula were brought to all subsequent Kings of France to be cured by the royal touch. Indeed, the only monarchs in Europe to be anointed with the pure chrism, instead of the ordinary sacred oil, were those of France and England, since from the time of the Hundred Years War **St Louis**'s female-line descendants the **Kings of England** claimed the throne of France and until the end of the **Stuart** dynasty also touched for the King's Evil.

For the **Valois** kings had to contend with the Hundred Years War, when the Kings of England – who were not even the nearest heirs female, as claimed – unjustly sought to wrest the crown of France from them. This was also a horrid time of civil strife. For example, among HRH's forebears, **Jean IV, Duke of Brittany** (the Breton-speaking Ancient Britons settled in Armorica) instigated **Pierre de Craon** in 1392 to attempt the assassination of **King Charles VI**'s commander-in-chief, **Olivier de Clisson, Constable of France**. When **John the Fearless, Duke of Burgundy** organised the slaying of **Louis, Duke of Orleans**: 'since the attempted murder of **Olivier de Clisson** the closest verification alone could guarantee the victim was undoubtedly dead'. So a man with a lighted straw checked and found all well: 'the right arm cut through in two places; the left wrist thrown to a distance, as if from the violence of the blow; the head open from ear to ear; the skull broken, and the brains scattered all over the pavement'. Later, **John the Fearless** in turn was cut down with a battle axe while attending a reconciliation conference with the sixteen-year-old **Dauphin** on the bridge at Montereau. But the young **Dauphin**, after Joan of Arc had him crowned as **King Charles VII** at Reims, set himself to bring peace to France. He was well served by the ministers he chose; and in 1453 his armies defeated and slew that veteran war-dog **John Talbot, Earl of Shrewsbury** at Castillon, when the English were at last driven out of all France save Calais alone. In his able administration, **Charles VII** was much influenced by lovely **Agnes Sorel**, who was 'the first to play a public and political role as mistress of a king of France, and may be said to have established a tradition'. Curiously enough, HRH descends from him both through **Agnes Sorel** and through his queen, **Marie of Anjou**, whose father belonged to the vigorous branch of the Capetian family reigning in Naples.

HRH's forebears include the great historian **Geoffroy de Villehardouin**, 'the first vernacular historian of France, and perhaps of modern Europe, who possesses literary merit'. HRH's most recent French ancestress was **Hyacinthe Gabrielle Roland, Marchioness Wellesley** (died 1816). But indeed, the names of HRH's earlier French ancestors read like a roll-call of the flower of the chivalry of France: **Montmorency** and **Guise**, **La Rochefoucauld** and **Rochechouart**, **Rohan** and **Polignac**, **Bauffremont** and **La Tour D'Auvergne**.

However, HRH's most popular French forefather

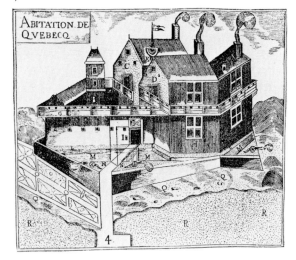

was probably **Henri IV, King of France** 1589–1610, the 'vert galant' or evergreen lover. He had previously been King of Navarre, and his famous exhortation 'suivez mon panache', referring to his plumed helmet, as he led his troops to victory at Ivry, has been well translated 'follow the white plumes of Navarre'. It was he who exclaimed 'Paris is worth a Mass'; and in his concern for the good of the peasantry and townsfolk, said it was his wish: 'every man a fowl in his pot'. During his reign, French Canada was much extended. Sadly, he was assassinated by a fanatic called Ravaillac, to France's great loss.

Quebec in 1608 under Henry IV, King of France, ancestor of HRH, whose grandmother is present Queen of Canada

Assassination of the Princess of Wales's ancestor King Henri IV in 1610

CHARLEMAGNE *(Charles the Great), Holy Roman Emperor of the West from 800, d.814*

Emperor LOUIS *the Pious, whose 'tastes were ecclesiastical rather than military', d.840*

Emperor CHARLES II *the Bald, suffered from Norman invaders, d.877*

LOUIS II *the Stammerer, K. of the West Franks, 'loved peace, justice and religion', d.879*

CHARLES *the Simple, K. of the West Franks, d.929 as prisoner of* HERIBERT, *Count of Vermandois*

LOUIS IV *d'Outremer, K. of the West Franks, d.954, held Laon with difficulty against* HUGH *the Great; m.* GERBERGA, *dau. of the German King* HENRY *the Fowler & sister of Emperor* OTTO *the Great*

MALTILDA *of France, Queen of Burgundy, d. after 982; m.* CONRAD *the Peaceful, K. of Burgundy, d.993*

GERBERGA *of Burgundy, Duchess of Swabia, living 988; m.* HERMANN II, *Duke of Swabia, d.1003*

GISELA *of Swabia, Empress, d.1043; m. Emperor* CONRAD II *the Salic, d.1039 (descended in female line from Emperor* OTTO *the Great)*

Emperor HENRY III *the Black, ruler of Germany, Italy & Burgundy, overlord of Hungary & Bohemia, d.1056*

Emperor HENRY IV, *'a friend of the lower orders', was obliged to submit to Pope Gregory the Great at Canossa, d.1106*

AGNES *of Germany, Duchess of Swabia, d.1143; m.* FREDERICK *of Hohenstaufen, Duke of Swabia, d.1105*

FREDERICK *'the One-Eyed' of Hohenstaufen, Duke of Swabia, d.1147 (m.* JUDITH, *of the House of* WELF*)*

Emperor FREDERICK *Barbarossa, accidentally drowned while on Crusade in Asia Minor 1190*

Earliest known portrait of Charlemagne, painted within a few years of his death

Emperor HENRY VI, *held Richard Coeur-de-Lion to ransom, d.1197 (m.* CONSTANCE, *heiress of the Norman kings of Sicily)*

Emperor FREDERICK II *'Stupor Mundi', K. of Sicily & Jerusalem, intellectual, introduced Arabic numerals, d.1250*

MANFRED *of Hohenstaufen, K. of Sicily, slain in battle against* CHARLES *of Anjou 1266*

CONSTANCE *of Hohenstaufen, Queen of Aragon & Sicily, d.1301; m.* PEDRO, *King of Aragon & Sicily, d.1285*

ELISABETH *of Aragon & Sicily, d.1336; m.* DINIZ, *K. of Portugal, d.1315*

ALFONSO IV, *K. of Portugal, d.1357*

PETER, *K. of Portugal, d.1367, made his courtiers do obeisance to the disinterred corpse of his murdered wife*

CONTINUED OVERLEAF

HRH's ancestor Emperor Maximilian I (1493–1519) with his wife Mary of Burgundy, and son Philip the Fair, and grandson Emperor Ferdinand, also HRH's ancestral uncles Emperor Charles V (opponent of the Reformation) and Louis II of Hungary

JOHN I, *K. of Portugal, d.1433*

DUARTE, *K. of Portugal, d.1438 (bro. of Henry the Navigator, organiser of African exploration)*

LEONORE *of Portugal, Empress, d.1476; m.* EMPEROR FREDERICK III *of Habsburg 1440–93 (descended from German King* RUDOLF *of Habsburg, d.1291)*

Emperor MAXIMILIAN I, *Archduke of Austria, Duke of Burgundy, 'last of the knights' but patron of scholars, d.1519*

PHILIP *of Habsburg, K. Consort of Spain, Archduke of Austria, d.1506*

Emperor FERDINAND I, *K. of Hungary & Bohemia, d.1564 (bro. of Emperor Charles V, 1519–56); m.* ANNE *of Bohemia (descended from German K.* ALBERT *of Habsburg d.1439 & Luxembourg Emperors)*

Archduchess JOHANNA *of Austria, d.1578 (sister of Emperor Maximilian II, a religious moderate); m.* FRANCESCO *de' Medici, Grand Duke of Tuscany, d.1587*

MARIE *de Medici, Queen of France, d.1642; m.* HENRI IV *de Bourbon, K. of France & Navarre, assassinated 1610*

HENRIETTA MARIA *of France, Queen of England, d.1669; m.* CHARLES I, *K. of England, beheaded 1649*

CHARLES II, *K. of Great Britain, the 'Merry Monarch', d.1685*

ancestors of HRH   *See Table 7*

BURKHARD *Count of Zollern, slain 1061 (probably scion of the Burkhardinger counts of Raetia c.900)*

FREDERICK I, *Count of Zollern, with his high stronghold at Hohenzollern in Swabia, living 1085–1115*

FREDERICK II, *Count of Zollern, powerful Swabian noble, d. c.1145*

FREDERICK I, *Burgrave of Nuremberg 1192–1200 (m.* SOPHIE *von Raabs, heiress of the burgraviate)*

CONRAD III, *Burgrave of Nuremberg 1201–61, administrator of Austria 1227*

FREDERICK III, *Burgrave of Nuremberg 1261–97, helped uncle* RUDOLF *of Habsburg to become German King*

FREDERICK IV, *Burgrave of Nuremberg 1300–32, 'saviour of the empire' at the battle of Mühldorf 1322*

JOHN II, *Burgrave of Nuremberg 1332–57, seized many robber-barons' fortresses as imperial fiefs*

FREDERICK V, *Burgrave of Nuremberg, Prince of the Holy Roman Empire from 1363, d.1398*

FREDERICK I, *Elector of Brandenburg from 1417, 'founder of the greatness of the House of Hohenzollern', d.1440*

ALBERT III, *'called* ACHILLES *for his knightly qualities', Elector of Brandenburg 1470–86*

JOHN *Cicero, Elector of Brandenburg, d.1499, eloquent Latin scholar, 'strove to improve the education of his people'*

JOACHIM I, *Elector of Brandenburg 1499–1535, from residence at Berlin protected his towns & industry*

JOACHIM II, *Elector of Brandenburg 1535–71, allowed the Lutherans free entrance but retained Catholic forms*

JOHN GEORGE, *Elector of Brandenburg 1571–98, made important financial economies in the State*

JOACHIM FREDERICK, *Elector of Brandenburg 1598–1608, Lutheran, administrator of Prussia from 1603*

JOHN SIGISMUND, *Elector of Brandenburg, d.1619 (m.* ANNA *of Hohenzollern, dau. of* ALBERT FREDERICK, *Duke in Prussia)*

GEORGE WILLIAM, *Elector of Brandenburg 1619–40, attempted unsuccessfully to remain neutral in the Thirty Years War*

FREDERICK WILLIAM, *'the Great Elector' of Brandenburg, Duke of Prussia, defeated Sweden, d.1688*

FREDERICK I, *K. in Prussia from 1701, as it lay outside Holy Roman Empire, d.1713*

FREDERICK WILLIAM I, *K. in Prussia 1713–40, reorganised his realm, & drove Sweden out of Pomerania*

Prince AUGUSTUS WM. *of Prussia, d.1758 (bro. of Frederick the Great, K. of Prussia from 1742, d.1786)*

FREDERICK WILLIAM II, *K. of Prussia 1786–97, took part in second & third Partitions of Poland*

FREDERICK WILLIAM III, *K. of Prussia 1797–1840, at first defeated by Napoleon, but took part in his overthrow*

CHARLOTTE *of Prussia, Empress* ALEXANDRA *of Russia d.1860 (sister of William, Emperor in Germany 1870–88); m.* NICHOLAS I, *Emperor of Russia, d.1855*

Grand Duke CONSTANTINE *Nicholaievich of Russia, General-Admiral, d.1892*

ancestors of HRH   *See Table 34*

LUITPOLD, *Margrave of Carinthia, Count in Bavaria (cousin & general of Emperor Arnulf) slain fighting Magyars 907*

BERCHTOLD, *Duke of Bavaria, d.947 (his elder bro. Duke Arnulf the Bad was candidate for imperial crown 919)*

HENRY, *Margrave at Schweinfurt in Bavaria, 10th century*

HENRY, *Count on the river Pegnitz in Bavaria, 11th century*

OTTO I, *Count on the river Paar c.1045, Vogt of Freising 1047, Count of Scheyern c.1070*

ECKEHARD I, *Count of Scheyern, d. c.1091*

OTTO IV *of Wittelsbach, imperial Count Palatine in Bavaria, built the castle of Wittelsbach 1124, d.1155*

OTTO V, *Duke of Bavaria from 1180, fought for Emperor FREDERICK Barbarossa, d.1183*

LUDWIG I, *Duke of Bavaria, crusader, Regent of Germany 1225–8, murdered at the bridge of Kelheim 1231*

OTTO *the Illustrious, Duke of Bavaria & Elector Palatine of the Rhine, imperial viceroy in Germany 1251–3*

LUDWIG II *the Severe, Duke of Bavaria & Elector Palatine, a candidate for imperial crown 1273, d.1294*

RUDOLF, *Duke of Upper Bavaria (bro. of Emperor LOUIS IV who d. suddenly at a bear hunt, 1347)*

ADOLPHUS *the Simple, Count Palatine of the Rhine, d.1327 (bro. of Elector Palatine Rudolf II the Blind)*

RUPERT *the Clement, German King 1400–10, Elector Palatine of the Rhine, 'brave & generous', d.1410*

STEPHEN, *Count Palatine at Simmern and Zweibruecken, d.1459*

FREDERICK I, *Count Palatine at Simmern and Zweibruecken, d.1480*

JOHN I, *Count Palatine at Simmern and Zweibruecken, d.1509*

JOHN II, *Count Palatine at Simmern and Zweibruecken, d.1557*

FREDERICK III *the Pious, Elector Palatine of the Rhine, 'one of the most active of the Protestant princes', d.1576*

LEWIS VI *the Facile, Elector Palatine of the Rhine, a Lutheran, d.1583*

FREDERICK IV *the Sincere, Elector Palatine of the Rhine, founder of the Evangelical Union, d.1610*

FREDERICK V, *the 'Winter King' of Bohemia, Elector Palatine of the Rhine, brought on Thirty Years War, d.1632*

CHARLES LEWIS, *Elector Palatine, d.1680 (bro. of the dashing Cavalier general, Prince Rupert of the Rhine)*

Raugräfin CAROLINE *Charlotte (morganatic daughter) d.1696; m.* MEINHARD, *Duke of Schomberg & Leinster (son of Marshal* FREDERIC, *Duke of Schomberg d. at battle of the Boyne)*

Lady FREDERICA *Schomberg, Countess of Holderness, d.1751; m.* ROBERT, *3rd Earl of Holderness, PC (descended from* THOMAS, *Ld. D'Arcy, beheaded in Pilgrimage of Grace)*

Lady CAROLINE *D'Arcy, Marchioness of Lothian, d.1778; m.* WILLIAM HENRY, *4th Marquess of Lothian, KT, General, wounded at Fontenoy 1745, d.1775*

Lady LOUISA *Kerr, d.1830; m. Lord* GEORGE HENRY *Lennox, d.1805*

CHARLES, *4th Duke of Richmond & Lennox, KG, Duc d'Aubigny, Govr.-Gen. of Canada, d. of a fox bite 1819*

CHARLES, *5th Duke of Richmond, KG (m.* CAROLINE, *dau. of Field-Marshal* HENRY, *Marquess of Anglesey, lost leg at Waterloo)*

Lady CECILIA CATHERINE *Gordon Lennox, Countess*
of Lucan, d.1910; m. GEORGE, *4th Earl of*
Lucan, d.1914 (son of Field-Marshal
GEORGE, *Earl of Lucan, commanded the*
Cavalry in Crimea)

Lady ROSALIND CECILIA *Bingham, Duchess of*
Abercorn; m. JAMES, *3rd Duke of Abercorn,*
KG, KP, *Govr. of N. Ireland, d.1953*

Lady CYNTHIA *Hamilton, Countess Spencer,* DCVO,
d.1972; m. JOHN, *7th Earl Spencer,*
wounded in First World War, d.1975

JOHN, *8th Earl Spencer, b.1924*

Lady DIANA *Spencer, Princess of Wales, b.1961; m.*
Prince CHARLES, *Prince of Wales, b.1948*

HRH

---

21 **SAXONY**
Wettin

BURKHARD, *Saxon count on the Sorbian March 892,*
d.908 (direct male line ancestor of HM QUEEN
ELIZABETH II)

grandfather of

DEDI, *Saxon count, 957*

DIETRICH I, *Saxon count 'of the Buzizi tribe', d.*
before 976

DEDI, *Count in the northern Hassegau 997, murdered*
1009

DIETRICH II, *Margrave of the East March of Saxony,*
murdered 1034 (m. MATILDE, *dau. of*
EKKEHARD, *Margrave of Meissen)*

THIMO, *Count of Brehna, d. c.1091*

THIMO *of Wettin, Margrave of Meissen 1103–04,*
built castle at Wettin that gave its name to
dynasty

CONRAD *the Great, Margrave of Meissen & Lusatia,*
also called the Pious, abdicated 1156, d.1157

OTTO *the Rich, Margrave of Meissen, d.1190*

DIETRICH I *the Exile, Margrave of Meissen &*
Lusatia, d.1221 (m. JUTTA, *dau. of*
HERMANN, *Landgrave of Thuringia)*

HENRY *the Illustrious, Margrave of Meissen &*
Landgrave of Thuringia (at war with HENRY
the Child of Hesse) d.1288

ALBERT II *the Degenerate, Landgrave of Thuringia,*
imprisoned by sons for a while, d.1314

FREDERICK I *the Undaunted, Landgrave of Thuringia,*
fought to recover Meissen, d.1323

FREDERICK II *the Grave, Landgrave of Thuringia &*
Margrave of Meissen, acquired several
counties, d.1349

FREDERICK III *the Strong, Landgrave of Thuringia &*
Margrave of Meissen (m. Countess
CATHERINE, *heiress of Coburg) d.1381*

FREDERICK I *the Warlike, Elector of Saxony from*
1423, with his capital at Wittenberg, d.1428

FREDERICK II *the Good, Elector of Saxony, d.1464*
(Saxony thenceforward divided between the
ERNESTINE & ALBERTINE *lines of his sons)*

ERNEST, *Elector of Saxony, d.1486 (his bro.* ALBERT
m. SIDONIA, *dau. of* GEORGE *of Poděbrad,*
K. of Bohemia)

JOHN *the Steadfast, El. of Saxony, d.1532 (bro. of*
Elector Fredk. the Wise, 'one of the most
illustrious princes of German history',
Reformation leader)

JOHN FREDERICK I *the Magnanimous, Elector of*
Saxony, d.1554, captured by Emperor
Charles V & forced to surrender the Electorate

Duke JOHN WM. *of Weimar (whose bro. John Fredk,*
Duke of Saxony, tried to recover Electorate
from Albertine cousins, but d. an imperial
prisoner)

CONTINUED OVERLEAF

JOHN *of Saxony, Duke of Weimar (i.e.*
    'Saxe-Weimar': Saxe being French for
    Saxony) d.1605

ERNEST *of Saxony, Duke of Gotha (i.e.*
    'Saxe-Gotha'), known as ERNEST *the Pious,*
    d.1675

JOHN ERNEST *of Saxony, Duke of Coburg (i.e.*
    'Saxe-Coburg'), d.1729

FRANCIS JOSIAS *of Saxony, Duke of Coburg (i.e.*
    'Saxe-Coburg'), d.1764

ERNEST FREDERICK *of Saxony, Duke of Coburg (i.e.*
    'Saxe-Coburg'), d.1800

FRANCIS *of Saxony, Duke of Coburg (i.e.*
    'Saxe-Coburg'), d.1806

ERNEST *of Saxony, reigning Duke of Coburg &*
    Gotha ('Saxe-Coburg-Gotha'), independent
    since end of Holy Roman Empire, d.1844

ALBERT *of Saxony, Prince Consort of Great Britain,*
    d.1861, helped to avert war with Federal
    Govt. in U.S. civil war

EDWARD VII, *K. of Great Britain & Ireland, Emperor*
    of India, d.1910, helped to found the 'Entente
    Cordiale'

GEORGE V, *K. of Great Britain & Ireland, Emperor of*
    India, d.1936, founded the Royal House of
    Windsor

GEORGE VI, *K. of Great Britain & Northern Ireland,*
    Emperor of India, d.1952, his Buckingham
    Palace was bombed by Nazis

Queen ELIZABETH II, *Head of the Commonwealth,*
    b.1926; m. Prince PHILIP, *Duke of*
    Edinburgh, b.1921

Prince CHARLES, *Prince of Wales, b.1948*

HRH

GERMANY & AUSTRIA

AT the time of the fall of the Western Roman Empire in the second half of the fifth century, the Teutonic nations of what became Germany had chosen their kings of sacral royal origin, mostly – like their Anglo-Saxon kinsmen who were engaged in conquering England – sprung from pagan kings who had incarnated the storm-spirit Woden or Wotan. There were five main tribes or nations, progenitors of the Saxons, Thuringians (whose ruling house incarnated Thor rather than Wotan), Swabians or Alamanns (hence 'Allemagne' as the French for Germany), Franks (whence Franconia) and Bavarians: though that was not yet their historic name.

Under HRH's forefathers **Charles Martel, King of the Franks** 737–41 and **King Pepin the Short** 751–68 (who probably had a descent from the Merovingian Woden-born *Cloderic the Parricide, King of Cologne,* murdered in 509), Christianity was accepted by all the Germans except the still heathen Saxons, whose conversion was effected in the next generation by **King Charles the Great** 768–814, who became the first **Holy Roman Emperor** as **Charlemagne** in 800. Under him, the whole area of what is now France and Germany, together with the Low Countries and northern Italy (Lombardy), were united in a single Frankish empire. But it soon split up into various kingdoms, among which the

West Franks formed France and the East Franks formed Germany. By the middle of the ninth century when HRH's ancestors, the half-brothers **Charles the Bold, King of the West Franks** and **Ludwig the German, King of the East Franks**, met to ratify an alliance, their courtiers were unable to understand each other's speech, so **King Charles** took the oath in a Romance, and **King Ludwig** in a Germanic dialect.

Thenceforward the Holy Roman Empire came in effect to mean Germany, although it long held suzerainty in northern Italy and elsewhere. The Emperors were always chosen from among the descendants of **Charlemagne**, in the male or female line, by the seven hereditary Great Officers of the Imperial Household, who eventually became known as the Prince Electors. The candidate elected became German King or 'King of the Romans' until his coronation by the Pope as Holy Roman Emperor: an event which sometimes never occurred during the long struggle for temporal domination of Germany and northern Italy between the Empire and the Papacy. By the Golden Bull of 1356, whose author was the **Emperor Charles IV**, it was settled that these seven Prince Electors should be the three Rhenish archbishops of Mainz, Cologne and Trier (as joint archchancellors), the **King of Bohemia** as arch-butler,

Seal of HRH's ancestor Godfried of Hohenlohe, Count of the Romagna, the earliest known to bear a date in Arabic numerals

the **Count Palatine of the Rhine** as arch-steward, the **Duke of Saxony** as arch-marshal and the **Margrave of Brandenburg** as arch-chamberlain. To these were added after the Thirty Years War the **Duke of Bavaria** (who got the Elector Palatine's job of arch-steward, with the latter compensated as arch-treasurer) and the **Duke of Brunswick** who became **Elector of Hanover**, first as arch-standard-bearer and later (when the Bavarian and Palatinate votes were united) as arch-treasurer. HRH descends from all these Electoral families.

Of HRH's ancestors who reigned in Germany after the Carolingian male line came to an end, two of the greatest were the **German King Henry the Fowler,** 919–36, and his son **Emperor Otto the Great**, 961–74, who brought the Danes to heel, utterly defeated the Magyar invaders, and under whom Germany began to feel collectively 'Deutsch'. Later arose the great **Hohenstaufen** dynasty, in which later legend confused the **Emperor Frederick Barbarossa**, accidentally drowned while on Crusade, with his grandson **Emperor Frederick II** 'the Wonder of the World', whose Court at Palermo as King of Sicily was one of the most cultivated there will ever have been, and far in advance of his time. He spoke six languages, tolerated Jewish and Mohammedan scholars, introduced Arabic numerals and algebra to Europe, founded the University of Naples, kept a zoo for the study of animals, and was interested in everything from poetry (the first sonnet was written at his Court) and architecture to medicine. He was sufficiently oriental, however, to keep a harem with eunuchs in attendance. When he was crowned Emperor by the Pope in 1220, he promised to go on crusade; and, although excommunicated by the next Pope who thought he had delayed through pretended sickness when in fact he had caught fever from his troops, **Frederick II** led the Sixth Crusade in which he skilfully managed through diplomacy instead of bloodshed, by negotiating with the Sultan of Egypt, the return to himself as **King of Jerusalem** of the towns of Nazareth and Bethlehem as well as the holy city of Jerusalem itself. Being still under the papal ban, this most remarkably successful of all crusaders was unable to be crowned there by a bishop, so he simply entered the Church of the Holy Sepulchre wearing his imperial crown. When he died, the Germans could not believe he was really gone for ever, and a legend (later transferred to his grandfather **Barbarossa**) tells how he sits asleep in a cave in the Kyffhäuser in front of a stone table through which his beard has grown, waiting for the time when a mighty horn will blow and he will awake to ride forth with his knights and restore to the Reich once more a golden age of peace.

Among this remarkable Emperor's most trusted advisers was the Franconian lord **Godfried of Hohenlohe**, whom he made **Count of the Romagna** and whose equestrian seal in 1237 is the earliest known seal in Christendom to bear a date in Arabic numerals. HRH descends from this **Count Godfried** many times over, but especially through **Heinrich-Friedrich, Count of Hohenlohe-Langenburg**, who died in 1699 and whose father **Count Philipp-Ernst of Hohenlohe** fought against the Turks in a suit of armour still preserved in their castle at Langenburg.

It would be impossible here to describe the deeds of all the other great German houses from whom HRH is descended, but among them such names as the **Wild-and-Rhinegraves**, the **Burgraves of Dohna**, **Erkinger lord of Schwarzenberg** and **Siegfried lord of Windisch-Graetz, Gotthard v. Metternich** and **Reinhard VIII v. Sickingen** and **Gundackar v. Starhemberg, Werner von der Schulenburg** (whose modern representative organised the Bomb Plot against Hitler) and even **Dietrich v. Münchhausen**, introduce us to families who were to make their mark on German history. Needless to say, such famous princely or county names as **Babenberg** (dukes of Austria before the Habsburgs), **Dietrichstein, Castell, Eltz, Eulenburg, Fürstenberg, Galen, Lodron,** the **count palatine Frederick the Victorious of Löwenstein, Mansfeld, Oettingen, Salm, Sayn-Wittgenstein, Stolberg, Thurn & Taxis, Thun** and **Trauttmansdorff** also appear in HRH's ancestry; as do the **Houses of Anhalt, Schleswig-Holstein, Lippe, Nassau, Olden-**

Philip, Landgrave of Hesse, soldier-statesman of the
Reformation (1504–67), ancestor of Prince Philip, Duke
of Edinburgh

burg, **Reuss**, **Schwarzburg** and **Waldeck**.

After the downfall of the Hohenstaufen: when **Charles of Anjou, King of the Two Sicilies** defeated and killed his predecessor, **Manfred of Hohenstaufen, King of the Two Sicilies** at the battle of Benevento in 1266 and two years later defeated and then publicly executed **Manfred**'s brother Conradin, last of the line, the principal families to come to the fore in the Holy Roman Empire were those of **Habsburg**, **Wittelsbach** and **Luxembourg**. Of these, **Rudolf, Count of Habsburg** was elected **German King** 1273–91, his son **Albert I** was **German King** 1298–1308, but the Habsburg family didn't secure the imperial crown again until **Albert V of Habsburg, Duke of Austria** became **German King** as **Albert II** in 1438. Meanwhile, the **Wittelsbach duke of Bavaria** became **Emperor Louis IV** 1314–47 and **Rupert of Wittelsbach, Elector Palatine of the Rhine** was elected **German King** 1400–10. But, throughout this period, it was the **Counts of Luxembourg** who provided the most notable emperors: among them HRH's forefathers the **Emperor Henry VIII**, 'a lover of Justice', whose premature death in 1313 was rumoured, probably without truth, to have been due to poison given him at Mass by a Dominican friar in the sacramen-

tal wine; also the much-loved **Emperor Charles IV** (died 1378) and the powerful **Emperor Sigismund** (died 1437), who both beautified Prague as their capital and for whom see the Czechs at Table 15 as they were also Kings of Bohemia.

After the **Emperor Sigismund**'s death the Electors turned to his heiress's husband, **Albert of Habsburg, Duke of Austria**, who became **German King** in 1438, as mentioned above, and thenceforward the House of Habsburg managed to become Emperors at almost every subsequent election until the dissolution of the Holy Roman Empire in 1806, following Napoleon's victory in the 'Battle of the Three Emperors' at Austerlitz. HRH descends from three of the next four Habsburg Emperors through both the **Prince** and **Princess of Wales**; in **Her Royal Highness**'s case by way of several different lines. These were the **Emperor Frederick III** (died 1493), the **Emperor Maximilian I** (died 1519), and the **Emperor Ferdinand I** (died 1564), whose elder brother, the Emperor Charles V, had been so burdened with the cares of state as ruler of Germany (including Austria), Spain, the Netherlands, Franche-Comté, Milan, Naples & Sicily and Sardinia, even Mexico and Peru, that he used to rehearse his own memorial Requiem Mass in Madrid while lying in his coffin.

Among HRH's imperial **Habsburg** forefathers, perhaps the most sympathetic character of all was that charming and fantastic dreamer, **Emperor Maximilian I**, 'the last of the knights', who, in his final, widowed, years contemplated taking Holy Orders and becoming Pope as well as Emperor. He was author of a number of books, some of them illustrated by Dürer himself; was patron of scholars and a talented linguist, interested in art, music and literature; 'enjoyed great popularity and rarely made a personal enemy'. An intrepid general in war and huntsman in peace, he introduced portable artillery and established standing forces; but when he was unable to raise troops in time to help the Holy League drive the French from Italy, the **Emperor** served personally with the English forces as a simple private volunteer and took part in their great victory in 1513 at the Battle of the Spurs. His marriage to **Mary**, heiress of **Charles the Bold, Duke of Burgundy**, perhaps the richest sovereign in Europe, brought the great wealth of the Netherlands (as well as the celebrated Order of the Golden Fleece) to the Habsburgs; and after **Juana, heiress of Spain**, married their son **Archduke Philip the Fair of Austria**, and **Anne, heiress of Bohemia & Hungary**, married their grandson the **Emperor Ferdinand I of Habsburg**, it was said in a famous Latin couplet *Alia bella gerunt sed tu felix Austria nubes*: 'Others wage wars, but you, happy Austria, marry.'

The Reformation started in Germany. The ablest soldier-statesman who made it possible was **Philip the Magnanimous, Landgrave of Hesse**, who signed the original Protest in 1529 from which the very word Protestant is derived; was the diplomatist whose skill organised the Schmalkaldic League of Protestant princes; and was then the brilliant artillery general who defeated the Catholic forces of the **German King Ferdinand I** (afterwards **Emperor**); but was later imprisoned for five years, 'and made to endure unspeakable hardships', after being captured by Spanish treachery. **Philip of Hesse**'s most remarkable achievement was perhaps to get both Luther and Melanchton to declare that there were plenty of precedents for more than one wife in the Old Testament and no direct prohibition in the New Testament, and to agree to his secret and morganatic *bigamous* second marriage: after which (in the words of his direct male-line descendant, HRH's great-granduncle Earl Mountbatten of Burma) the **Landgrave Philip** 'divided his time discreetly between his wives, **Cristina**, who lived ceremoniously mostly at Cassel, bearing him a further three children, and Margaret, who lived in seclusion mostly at Spangenberg, bearing him nine children'.

During the seventeenth century, Germany was devastated by the religious horrors of the Thirty Years War, which began with the expulsion from Bohemia of HRH's ancestor the **'Winter King'**, and ended in 1648 with the establishment of the simple dictum *cujus regio ejus religio:* by which each state adopted the faith of its ruler. The worries of this period were epitomised by the policies of another of HRH's forefathers, **John George, Elector of Saxony** 1611–56, who found himself at different times in alliance with or fighting against the Catholic imperial forces and the Protestant invading Swedes. When the war was over, Germany settled down in various states under the nominal rule of the Habsburg emperors until the dissolution of the Holy Roman Empire in 1806.

After 1806, these states were independent until the establishment of the German empire in 1870. Thus HRH's recent ancestors included **Frederick Eugene, Duke of Württemberg** (died 1797), whose eldest son became first King of Württemberg; **Charles Frederick, reigning Grand Duke of Baden**, whose reign was the longest in modern history, starting as Margrave in 1738, taking the

John George I, Elector of Saxony 1611–56, HRH's Albertine ancestor

title of Elector in 1803 and Grand Duke in 1806, before dying at last in 1811, and whose Zähringen dynasty sprang in the direct male line from **Berchtold, Count in the Breisgau** in 962; **Charles II, reigning Grand Duke of Mecklenburg-Strelitz** (died 1816), descended from the only Slav sovereign dynasty in Germany, from the pagan **Prince Niklot of the Obotrites** who was slain in battle against the Saxons in 1160; **George of Brunswick, King of Hanover** (better known as **King George III of Great Britain**, died 1820), sprung in the direct male line from **Adalberto, Marquis of Este** in Italy in 915; **Augustus of Saxony, reigning Duke of Gotha** (died 1822), **Ernest of Saxony, reigning Duke of Coburg** (died 1844) and **Joseph of Saxony, reigning Duke of Altenburg** (abdicated 1848); **Louis III, reigning Grand Duke of Hesse and the Rhine** (died 1877), ancestor of the Mountbattens and descended in the direct male line from the Belgian

HRH's ancestral uncle Frederick the Great, King of Prussia (1740–86)

Landgrave Louis VIII of Hesse-Darmstadt (1739–68), ancestor of the Mountbattens, in his stag chariot

count Gisilbert on the Meuse, who kidnapped and married **Charlemagne**'s great-granddaughter **Irmgard** in 846; and, above all in this context, **Frederick William III**, **King of Prussia** (died 1840), father of the first German Emperor.

For the **Kings of Prussia** eventually ousted the Habsburgs in the contest to be the dynasty that was to re-unify Germany. The **Hohenzollerns** came to the fore under **Frederick William, the 'Great Elector' of Brandenburg** 1640–88, founder of the Prussian army, who was called by a French observer 'the sharpest fox in Europe'. He was **Duke of Prussia** by descent from **Anna of Hohenzollern**, whose grandfather **Duke Albert** had been the last *Hochmeister* of the famous junker Teutonic Knights (originally crusaders against the pagan Slavs) to rule in Prussia but had abandoned his vows of celibacy to become Lutheran sovereign duke there instead. Since Prussia lay outside the Holy Roman Empire, the **Great Elector**'s son **Frederick** was able to take the title of 'King in Prussia' in 1701. An old nobleman once told a Prus-

sian king that his own ancestors had been in the Mark of Brandenburg long before the Hohenzollerns arrived there. 'But we've got on further,' replied the king.

This title was firmly changed to King of Prussia by Frederick the Great who, although childless himself, was HRH's ancestral uncle. Like his cousin **King George III of Great Britain**, Frederick the Great probably inherited that painful hereditary malady porphyria from **Mary Queen of Scots**, though in a less acute form. He was one of the most remarkable monarchs in HRH's family tree. Popular, a highly skilled flute-player, philosopher, wit, soldier – 'Dogs, would you live for ever?' he once shouted at some troops who were panicking under heavy fire – diplomatist, economist and legal reformer: he considered it his duty to be 'the advocate of the poor'. His grand-nephew, **Frederick William III, King of Prussia** 1797–1840, 'beloved by his subjects, who valued him for the simplicity of his manners and the goodness of his heart', was, as we have seen, the father of HRH's ancestral uncle William I, first German Emperor when in 1870 the Second Reich was formed to unite Germany once again.

ÁLMOS, *chosen as best of the 7 Magyar nomad princes to be chief and to have the honour of being sacrificed before they set out for Europe*

ÁRPAD, *Duke of the Magyars, led emigration from Dnieper steppes 889 to conquer Hungary & Transylvania by 895, d.907*

ZSOLTÁN, *Duke of Hungary, d.947, defeated by Saxons 933 near Merseburg while invading Germany; m. Khazar princess, dau. of* MAROT, *Khagan of Jewish Khazars between rivers Theiss & Szamos*

TAKSONY, *Duke of Hungary, d.972, whose army was defeated by* OTTO *the Great 955 near Augsburg*

MICHAEL, *Magyar prince (uncle of St Stephen, first K. of Hungary in the millenium year 1000)*

VÁSZOLY, *pagan Magyar prince, imprisoned & blinded by K. Stephen before 1038, and his sons exiled to Poland*

BELA I, *K. of Hungary 1061–3 (defeated & slew his bro. K. Andrew I, who had tried to alter the succession)*

GEYSA I, *K. of Hungary 1074–77, 'righteous and generous', overthrew his unjust cousin K. Salomon in battle*

ÁLMOS, *Duke of Croatia, d.1129, blinded (with his son) by his bro., K. Kálmán of Hungary*

BELA II, *blind K. of Hungary 1131–41, whose wife avenged his blindness by slaying in the Diet his former opponents*

GEYSA II, *K. of Hungary 1141–61, long at war with his Byzantine cousin, Emperor Manuel Comnenus*

BELA III, *K. of Hungary 1173–96, 'one of the most powerful and respected rulers', brought up at the Byzantine Court; m.* AGNES, *dau. of the ferocious crusader* RENAUD *of Châtillon beheaded by Saladin in person 1187*

ANDREW II, *K. of Hungary 1205–35, forced to issue the Golden Bull, 'the Magna Carta of Hungary' 1222*

BELA IV, *K. of Hungary 1235–70, 'man of genius', gave refuge to the Kuns (Cumans), was overrun by the Mongols 1241*

STEPHEN V, *K. of Hungary 1270–72, successfully resisted invasion by K.* OTTAKAR *of Bohemia; m.* ELISABETH, *baptised dau. of* KUTYEN, *Khan of the Kuns (Cumans) murdered by suspicious Magyars 1241*

MARY *of Hungary, Queen of Naples, d.1323 (sister of Ladislas IV, K. of Hungary 1272–90); m.* CHARLES II, *K. of Naples, d.1309*

BLANCA *of Naples, Queen of Aragon, d.1310 (aunt of 'Carobert', K. of Hungary 1310–42); m.* JAMES II, *K. of Sicily 1285–96, K. of Aragon 1291–1327*

ALFONSO IV, *K. of Aragon 1327–36*

PEDRO IV, *K. of Aragon 1336–87*

ELEANOR *of Aragon, Queen of Castile, d.1382; m.* JOHN I, *K. of Castile 1379–90*

HENRY III, *K. of Castile 1390–1406*

JOHN II, *K. of Castile 1406–54*

ancestors of the Habsburgs and of HRH   See Table 7

The crown 'of St. Stephen' worn by HRH's Árpad ancestors, Hungary's most treasured relic

HUNGARY

THE Magyars were nomads from central Asia moving westwards and established on the steppes between the Don and the Dnieper, when in 889 they were defeated and driven from their then feeding grounds by the Petchenegs, who in turn were pressing on them from the East. So the Magyars resolved on mass emigration. They were of course still pagan, although they believed in an ultimate godhead, Isten, 'creator of all created things'. Their shamanist priests divined auguries from the burnt shoulder-blades of sacrificed animals, and on very solemn occasions they sacrificed white horses: a custom rumoured to be kept up secretly in oak groves on occasions as late as the seventeenth century.

But the crisis of 889 called for a supreme sacrifice. The princes of the seven Magyar clans met together and chose prince **Álmos**, as the senior and best among the seven, to be chief of all the Magyars. Cutting open the veins of their arms, the princes each drank the mingled blood of all, and took five vows, of which the first was that 'As long as they and their progeny after them shall live, their duke and ruler shall be always taken from the house of **Álmos**.' Then they offered up **Álmos** himself as an honoured and willing sacrifice of the very best possession they had; prayed to Isten for the success of their migration; and then set off under their new **Duke Árpad**, son of the sacrificed **Duke Álmos**, to conquer the Great Plain of Hungary or die in the attempt.

They succeeded. In 894, **Duke Árpad** completely defeated the great Duke of Moravia, and soon afterwards the entire Magyar nation had subjugated what is now Hungary, Transylvania and Slovakia. Attempts to invade Germany itself were unsuccessful. In 933, **King Henry the Fowler** routed **Duke Zsoltán** at Merseburg in spite of the Saxon Christian war-cry of 'Kyrie eleison' being answered by the Magyar battle-yell of 'Hooy, Hooy!'; and in 955 the army sent by **Duke Taksony** was so soundly defeated by **Emperor Otto the Great** near Augsburg that only seven Magyars escaped back to Hungary, where they were publicly disgraced.

Under St Stephen, HRH's ancestral first cousin, Hungary became officially Christian, though paganism lingered on for some time. In the year of the Christian millenium, 1000, with imperial agreement, the Pope sent St Stephen a crown and an Apostolic cross, and he became the first of the

Apostolic Kings of Hungary. This famous crown has been Hungary's most treasured relic ever since, although it was added to by HRH's royal **Árpad** ancestors who inherited and wore it: the Byzantine circlet which forms the lower part of the crown was sent in about 1075 to HRH's ancestor **King Geysa I** by Emperor Michael VII, son of another of HRH's forefathers, the **Emperor Constantine XI**, and seems to have been united to the closed original upper part for **King Bela IV**, who pulled Hungary together after the Mongol destruction of 1241–2. The regalia underwent many adventures, and the special retention of an accidental tilting of the Cross that surmounts it makes the Crown of St Stephen unmistakable.

Bela IV indeed guided Hungary through one of the greatest crises of her history. In 1221 a Mongol cavalry army under command of two of **Genghis Khan**'s best generals had made a reconnaissance in force into eastern Europe. On the way, they had passed northwards through the Caucasian Mountains and encountered opposition from the warrior horsemen of **Kutyen, Khan of the Cumans** or Kuns, themselves shamanist Turko-Mongol nomads who controlled the steppes above the Sea of Azov. **Genghis Khan**'s generals bought off the Cumans, and then secretly followed them, recovering the booty and slaying **Kutyen Khan**'s brother and son. The Cuman khan then made an alliance with the princes of southern Russia, especially HRH's other ancestors **Mstislav the Daring, Prince of Galicia** (Halicz) and **Daniel, Prince of Volynia**, but were again defeated by the Mongol generals: the Prince of Kiev being captured. That night the two Mongol generals dined on a box-shaped table inside which the captured Prince of Kiev and two other Russian princes were gradually suffocating to death: this was done out of respect, as 'by Mongol tradition no man was worthy to shed the blood of a prince except in battle'. When the main Mongol armies began a new invasion in 1238, **Kutyen Khan** took refuge in Hungary with 40,000 Cuman warriors and their families, was converted to Christianity, and married his daughter to **King Bela IV**'s son, the future **King Stephen V**, bringing more Asiatic blood into HRH's ancestry. But many Magyars mistrusted him, and, when the Mongols invaded Hungary in 1241, some Hungarian lords massacred poor **Kutyen Khan**, together with his household, at his quarters in Pesth. It was left to **Bela IV** to restore Hungary to peace and order after the Mongols withdrew.

After the male line of the House of Árpad came to an end in 1301, Hungary was ruled by various kings, among them HRH's direct ancestors the **Emperor Sigismund of Luxembourg, King of Hungary** 1387–1437, **Albert of Habsburg, King of Hungary** 1437–9, **Ulászló II Jagiellon, King of Hungary** 1490–1516 (known as King Dobře', the yes-man) and the **Emperor Ferdinand of Habsburg, King of Hungary** 1527–64. This was the period of the wars with Turkey, and in 1566 HRH's forefather **Nicholas, Count Zrinyi**, Ban of Croatia, was hero of one of the most famous episodes in Hungarian history. Hopelessly besieged in Szigetvár by a vast Turkish army under Suleiman the Magnificent, the gallant **Zrinyi** lowered the drawbridge and charged out to certain death, not knowing that the sultan was dead in his tent, secretly embalmed by his grand vizier. The next sultan, Selim the Sot, sent to Vienna as a present for the emperor **Count Zrinyi**'s pickled head, with his fur cap, ornamented with a heron's plume and diamond rosettes, still fixed to his skull by a Turkish arrow.

Other famous Hungarian names abound in HRH's ancestry: **Perényi de Perény** and **Bethlen de Bethlen**, **Forgách de Gács** and **Thelegdy de Thelegd**, **Thurzó de Bethlenfalva**, **Balassa** and **Lónyay de Nagy-Lónya**; and **Thomas, Count Széchy** who died in 1618.

But it was perhaps in Transylvania that HRH's Magyar ancestors played thereafter their most important role. Already, in 1432, HRH's ancestor **Stephen Báthory** had been Vice-Voivode of Transylvania. The constant wars made people a bit rough. Thus in 1514, rootless peasants, armed for a crusade, had instead ravaged the Great Plain of Hungary, pillaging and burning, massacring by 'crucifixion and other unspeakable methods' thousands of Magyar gentry including the Lord Treasurer Thelegdy, tortured before being hung up naked on a tree and finished off with arrows. This was too much: so HRH's ancestral uncle John Zapolyai, Voivode of Transylvania rode north with the mounted yeomanry of Transylvania; and the revolting peasantry were crushed. John Zapolyai had a Gilbertian sense of 'making the punishment fit the crime', and made a startling example of the ringleaders. 'The rebel leaders,

including Dózsa, were thrown into prison, and were not permitted to taste any food for a fortnight. Nine of them still remained amongst the living. Dózsa was seated on a red hot iron throne, a red hot iron crown was placed on his forehead, and a red hot sceptre forced into his hand. Not a murmur of pain escaped him during this dreadful torture. Only when his famished companions in arms rushed upon him and tore the charred flesh from his body to appease their craving for food, he exclaimed: "These are hounds of my own choosing".'

After the tragic death of HRH's ancestral uncle Ulászló I, King of Hungary on the fatal field of Mohács, the decisive Turkish victory in 1526, HRH's ancestor **Ferdinand of Habsburg** claimed the throne and established himself as the new **King of Hungary** at Poszony (Pressburg, now Bratislava); but the majority of the nobles meanwhile had elected and crowned HRH's other ancestral uncle John Zapolyai, King of Hungary 1526–40 instead, and the Sultan installed him in Buda, so that there were rival kings in the east and the west until King John Zapolyai's death. HRH descends from his sister **Barbara Zapolyai, Queen of Poland**: they were the children of **Stephen Zapolyai, Lord Palatine of Hungary**.

Until 1556 Transylvania had been administered by Voivodes appointed by the Crown, but as a result of the Turkish conquest of much of Hungary, Transylvania became a sovereign country with its own elected Princes until 1699, when it became customary to elect the Habsburg kings of Hungary in that office. HRH's ancestor **John Kemény, Prince of Transylvania** died in 1662, while **Michael Barcsay de Nagy-Barcsa** was half-brother of Ákos Barcsay, Prince of Transylvania 1658–61; and another forefather, **Paul Rhédey de Kis-Rhéde**, was uncle of Francis Rhédey, Prince of Transylvania, who died in 1658. HRH's most recent Hungarian ancestress was the young and beautiful **Countess Claudine Rhédey**, who died as the result of a fall from her horse in 1841, daughter of **László, Count Rhédey** and created **Countess von Hohenstein** in her own right on her morganatic marriage in Vienna to the royal **Duke Alexander of Württemberg**. Her son **Francis, Duke of Teck**, GCB, was father of **Queen Mary**, wife of **King George V of Great Britain, Emperor of India**.

23 **ITALY:** FLORENCE
Medici

GIOVANNI *dei Medici, 1360–1429, Florentine banker, amassed an immense fortune*

COSIMO *'the Elder' dei Medici, d.1464, called 'Pater Patriae', effective ruler of Florence in private*

PIERO *'the Gouty' dei Medici, d.1464, effective ruler of Florence (his yr. son Giulio was father of Pope Clement VII)*

LORENZO *'the Magnificent' dei Medici, d.1492, under whom Florence reached her artistic zenith*

LUCREZIA *dei Medici, d. c.1550 (sister of Pope Leo X); m.* GIACOMO *Salviati, patrician of Florence, d.1533*

MARIA *Salviati, d.1543; m.* GIOVANNI *'the Invincible' dei Medici (Giovanni delle Bande Nere), brilliant Papal Capt.-Gen., slain 1526*

COSIMO I *dei Medici, Grand Duke of Tuscany 1537–74, 'an absolute prince who was likewise a statesman of eminent ability'*

FRANCESCO *dei Medici, Grand Duke of Tuscany 1574–87, devoted to science & letters, founded Uffizi gallery*

MARIE *de' Medici, Queen of France, d.1642; m.* HENRI *IV, K. of France, assassinated 1610*

HENRIETTA MARIA *of France, Queen Consort of England, d.1669*

ancestors of HRH   *See Tables 17 & 18*

24 **ITALY:** MILAN
Visconti

MATTEO I *Visconti, Lord of Milan 1295–1322, Imperial Vicar of Lombardy (nephew of Ottone Visconti, Archbp. of Milan 1262)*

STEFANO *Visconti, d.1327 (bro. of Galeazzo I, Ld. of Milan d.1328, and Lucchino, Ld. of Milan, poisoned by his wife 1349); m.* VALENTINA, *dau. of* BERNABO *Doria, joint Captain of People of Genoa 1306–9*

BERNABO *Visconti, Lord of Milan (with bro.* GALEAZZO II, *assassinated immoral elder bro. Matteo II), d.1385; m.* BEATRICE, *dau. of* MASTINO II *della Scala, Lord of Verona (& sister of* CANGRANDE II *della Scala)*

CATERINA *Visconti, d.1404; m. cousin* GIAN GALEAZZO I, *Duke of Milan 1346–1402, captured Verona, Padua, Siena & Bologna*

VALENTINA *Visconti, Duchess of Orleans, 'beautiful and accomplished', d.1408; m.* LOUIS *of Valois, Duke of Orleans, murdered by Burgundians 1407*

CHARLES, *Duke of Orleans, severely wounded at Agincourt 1415, d.1465*

JOHN, *Count of Angoulême, d.1467*

CHARLES, *Count of Angoulême, d.1496*

MARGUERITE *of Angoulême, Queen of Navarre, d.1549 (sister of François I, K. of France); m.* HENRI II *d'Albret, K. of Navarre, d.1555*

JEANNE *d'Albret, Queen of Navarre, d.1572*

ancestors of HRH   *See Table 17*

The Princess of Wales's forefather Lorenzo the
Magnificent dei Medici (1449–92) from the fresco in the
Gozzoli chapel in Florence

FRANCESCO *Sforza, Duke of Milan 1450–66, brilliant condottiere general, maintained great splendour*

CATERINA *Sforza, brave Countess of Forli (natural daughter), outraged by Cesare Borgia while his prisoner, d.1509; m. secretly* GIULIANO *dei Medici, Florentine ambassador at her Court, who d.1498*

GIOVANNI *'delle Bande Nere' dei Medici, Papal Capt.-Gen. for Medici Pope Clement* VII, *slain in battle, d.1525*

ancestors of HRH   *See Table 23*

Prince Charles's ancestor Bartolomeo Colleoni, Captain-General of the Venetian forces 1455–75, whose equestrian statue by Verrocchio is still one of the treasured sights of Venice

ITALY

HRH descends from Charlemagne's son **Pepin, King of Italy** 781–810, and from his Carolingian successors: **Bernard, King of Italy** 814–17, **Emperor Louis the Debonnaire, King of Italy** 817–40, **Emperor Lothair** I, **King of Italy** 840–55, **Emperor Louis** II, **King of Italy** 855–75, and **Emperor Charles the Bald, King of Italy** 875–6. More than a century later, HRH's forefather **Alberto Azzo** II, **Marquis of Italy** for the Holy Roman Empire, inherited the town of **Este** from his mother **Valdrada**, daughter of **Pietro Candiano** IV, **Doge of Venice** by a granddaughter of **Hugh of Arles, King of Italy** 926–45, a relation of the disreputable Papal 'pornocracy' of the tenth century. **King Hugh**'s successor King Lothair left a young and beautiful widow, **Queen Adelheid**, who was imprisoned on a sunny island in Lake Como by HRH's ancestor **Berengar** II, **Marquis of Ivrea** (descended of the **Dukes of Spoleto** and the heiress of the **Counts of Friuli**) who had become **King of Italy** and was anxious to keep it an independent nation. To this end, **King Berengar** tried to force her into marriage with his son **Adalberto, co-King of Italy**; but **Queen Adelheid** escaped to safe refuge in the castle of Canossa, and then married instead the future **Emperor Otto the Great**, who entered Lombardy in 961, deposed **Berengar** and **Adalberto**, and assumed the crown in Milan as **King of Italy** himself. Thenceforward the Holy Roman Emperors, as overlords of Lombardy, considered themselves titular Kings of Italy.

The Emperors soon clashed with the Papacy over the eternal problem of separating temporal and spiritual authority: the adherents of the emperor being nicknamed the Ghibellines and those of the pope the Guelphs. With that genealogical and indeed multi-racial impartiality that properly betokens the Blood Royal, HRH descends from both sides in the long struggle between the **Guelphs** and **Ghibellines** in Italy.

Meanwhile, despite imperial suzerainty in the north, seven powers emerged in Italy: Savoy, the Papal States, Venice, Genoa, Florence, Milan and the kingdom of the Two Sicilies (Naples and Sicily). Two vigorous Norman brothers, both ancestors of HRH and sons of **Tancred de Hauteville** in Normandy, had established themselves in the south of Italy: the elder being the celebrated **Robert Guiscard, Duke of Apulia and Calabria, Prince of Salerno**, who sacked Rome for three days in 1084, from whom HRH descends through his famous crusader son **Bohemund, Prince of Antioch**; and the younger brother being **Roger** I, **the 'Great Count' of Sicily**, who conquered that huge island from the Saracens with a handful of mailed Norman knights between 1061 and 1091. **Count Roger**'s son **Roger** II succeeded to Apulia as well, reduced Naples and Capua to order, and was crowned as **Roger, King of the Two Sicilies** at Palermo on Christmas Day 1130, making Sicily the leading maritime power in the Mediterranean. 'The Capella Palatina, at Palermo, the most wonderful of **King Roger**'s churches, with Norman doors, Saracenic arches, Byzantine dome, and roof adorned with Arabic scripts, is perhaps the most striking product of the brilliant and mixed civilisation over which the Norman **Tancred** ruled.' His daughter **Constance, Queen of Sicily** 1195–8, married the **Emperor Henry VI of Hohenstaufen**, and their son **Emperor Frederick II, King of Sicily** 1198–1250, the 'Wonder of the World', made Palermo the most brilliant Court in Europe. For HRH's descent from this very remarkable sovereign, see Table 18.

But **Frederick II**'s natural son **King Manfred** was defeated and slain at Benevento in 1266 by the Capetian **Charles of Anjou, King of the Two Sicilies** 1266–85, to whom this Ghibelline crown had been granted by the Guelph party pope, and who made Naples his capital. But, Angevin foreign oppression soon welded the island of Sicily into a nation; and a pass made by a Frenchman at an attractive Sicilian woman led to the grim Sicilian Vespers, when the predecessors of the Mafia rose up and massacred everybody who couldn't pronounce the Italian word *ciceri* correctly: rather like 'shibboleth' in the Bible Story. After **King Manfred** had been slain at Benevento, the Angevins had also defeated and 'executed' his brother Conradin, whose glove was sent to **Manfred**'s daughter and heiress **Constance, Queen of Aragon**. The challenge was taken up, and the royal **House of Aragon** recovered first Sicily, also eventually Naples too: HRH descending through the **Princess of Wales** from **Federigo of Aragon, King of Naples**, deposed in 1501 by a French invasion at the invitation of Pope Alexander VI Borgia when the Guelph party once again overcame the Ghibellines.

In the north, the Dukes of Savoy ruled over Piedmont. They descended from **Umberto III the White-Handed, Count of Savoy**, who had been Count of Salmourenc in France, had extended his power to the Lake of Geneva by 1017, and to the Val d'Aosta in Italy by 1024. He thus controlled three great Alpine passes (Mount Cenis and the two St Bernards) and his son **Count Oddone** acquired Piedmont by marriage to **Adelaide**, heiress of Turin, descendant of **Ardoino Glabrione of Ivrea, Marquis of Italy** 942–72 for the Empire. HRH's descent from their own descendant, **Philip II, Duke of Savoy** (died 1497) is given at Table 14. His elder brother **Amadeus IX, Duke of Savoy**

1465–72, was also HRH's ancestor.

Through the House of Savoy, HRH descends quite lawfully from a Pope. In 1434, **Amadeus VIII, Duke of Savoy**, 'distinguished for his wisdom and justice', handed over the sovereign duchy to his son **Louis** and retired to a hermitage by the Lake of Geneva. Five years later, as he was a widower and despite his not being a priest, **Duke Amadeus** was elected pope by the Council of Basel, and crowned with the papal tiara in 1440 as **Pope Felix V**. Ancestral uncles of HRH to have held the papacy include Pope Gregory V 996–9 (brother of **Henry, Count of Speyer**), Pope Leo IX 1048–54 (brother of **Gerard III, Count of Egisheim**), Pope Stephen IX 1057–8 (brother of **Godfrey the Bearded, Duke of Lower Lorraine**), Pope Calixtus II 1119–24 (brother of **Raymond, Count of Burgundy**), Pope Celestine III 1191–8 (brother of **Urso Orsini**), Pope Innocent IV 1243–53 (brother of **Obizzo di Fiesco**), Pope Nicholas III 1277–80 (brother of **Gentile Orsini**) and Pope Leo X (brother of **Maddelena dei Medici**): it was HRH's ancestral first cousin, Pope Clement VII dei Medici, 1523–34, who had that beautiful Renaissance bathroom, one of the earliest in Christendom, painted in the Castel San Angelo in Rome.

But perhaps HRH's most hallowed ancestral uncle in Italy at this period was St Thomas Aquinas (c.1227–74), whose brother **Adenolfo, Count of Aquino**, with his castle at Roccasecca near Naples, was ancestor through the **Counts of Celano, Areano, Nola** and **St Pol**, of **Jacqueline of Luxembourg, Countess Rivers**, whose daughter **Lady Elizabeth Wydeville** married **King Edward IV of England**. These Counts of Nola were Orsini, and HRH also descends from **Raimundello Orsini, Prince of Taranto and Count of Lecce** (died 1406), son of **Nicola Orsini, Senator of Rome** 1356, and thus the famous Roman senatorial **Orsini**: the House of the Bear.

Independent walled cities were becoming powers in Italy: in particular the great maritime powers of Genoa and Venice. HRH's most historic Genoese descents are perhaps those through **Bernabo Doria, joint Captain of the People of Genoa** 1306–9, and his then colleague **Opiccino Spinola**, afterwards sole **Captain of the People of Genoa** 1309–10: those were the days when the Doria and Spinola, who were Ghibellines, fought for control of Genoa against the Fieschi (descended from HRH's ancestor **Obizzo di Fiesco**) and the Grimaldi, who belonged to the Guelph party. In Venice, founded as an Italian refuge in the Rialto lagoons by Venetians determined to adhere to the

Byzantine Roman empire and not to submit to the Frankish new-fangled Holy Roman Emperor's son **Pepin, King of Italy** 781–810, HRH descends from some of the greatest early doges: among them **St Pietro Orseole I, Doge of Venice** 976–8, who began the rebuilding of St Mark's in the Piazza San Marco after a disastrous fire, before leaving Venice secretly to die a monk and eventually to be canonised; and his son **Pietro Orseole II, Doge of Venice** 991–1009, 'one of the chief founders of the commercial greatness of Venice'. His foundation of the Venetian fleet and decisive victory over the Adriatic pirates in their swift Liburnian vessels made him **Duke of Dalmatia**, and was thenceforward commemorated in that magnificent annual ceremony where each successive doge threw a symbolic ring overboard from the dogal barge *Bucentaur* in the 'wedding of the Sea'. But perhaps the most renowned doge of all from whom HRH descends was the great **Enrico Dandolo, Doge of Venice** 1192–1205, who, aged over eighty and almost blind, commanded the fleet of the diverted Latin crusader army that took Constantinople from the Byzantine Greeks in 1204, and then sacked it, acquiring Crete for Venice and bringing back the famous four bronze horses which so adorn St Mark's (see Table 11).

And rather a surprising ancestor of HRH was **Bartolomeo Colleoni, Captain-General of the Venetian Forces** 1455–75, 'perhaps the most respectable of all the Italian *condottieri*'. Another surprising *condottiere* forefather of HRH was **Sir John Hawkwood, Captain-General of the Florentine Forces** 1390–4, the most modern general of his time, who led his White Company of English mercenaries into Italy, served both for and against the Papacy and Milan, and married a Visconti bastard, before settling down in a villa near Florence, where his portrait in terre-verte by Paolo Uccelli is preserved in the cathedral.

Those early days of the Italian renaissance saw a flowering of the arts in the various city states where HRH's ancestors held their brilliant Courts. Among these forefathers were the House of Este down to **Nicolo III d'Este, Marquis of Ferrara, Modena and Parma**, poisoned as Governor of Milan in 1441; that of Carrara down to **Francesco III 'Novello' da Carrara, Prince of Padua**, strangled in 1406 while a prisoner of war in Venice; the

talented Gonzaga down to **Federigo I Gonzaga, Marquis of Mantua**, simultaneously a fine patron of the arts and an able soldier, who died in 1484; the splendidly sinister Malatesti down to **Galeotto-Roberto Malatesta, Lord of Rimini** (died 1432), whose incredible brother Sigismondo Malatesta of Rimini figured remarkably during the Renaissance, 'of which indeed he was one of the strangest and most original representatives'; and the tragic Scaligeri down to **Cangrande II della Scala, Lord of Verona** 1351–9, and his natural son **Guglielmo della Scala, Lord of Verona** (died 1404) who fathered a line in exile down to **Hans della Scala, Herr v. Bern** (died 1541) – HRH's Scaliger ancestral uncle Cangrande I had been the patron of Dante.

The eventual conquest of Verona by the Visconti brings us to HRH's Milanese ancestry, for which see Tables 24 & 25. HRH's Visconti ancestors bore the dread battle-banner of a Viper devouring a Child, and lived up to that horrible device. But the brothers **Galeazzo II Visconti, Lord of Pavia**, where he founded the university and was the patron of Petrarch, and **Bernabo, Lord of Milan** were highly civilised rulers. Nevertheless, **Bernabo** was put to death in 1385 by his nephew and son-in-law **Gian Galeazzo Visconti, Duke of Milan** 1396–1402, who built the magnificent cathedral at Milan. The dynasty's claim to Milan eventually passed through **Duke Gian Galeazzo I**'s sister **Valentina Visconti, Duchess of Orleans** to the Royal House of France. In the meantime, however, the famous *condottiere* general **Francesco Sforza** had succeeded as **Duke of Milan** 1450–66, and his natural daughter **Caterina Sforza, Countess of Forli**, brave and clever, made her mark on Italian history before being captured after a gallant defence of Forli and raped by Cesare Borgia.

Caterina Sforza's secret husband was **Giuliano dei Medici**, and their son, the great soldier **Giovanni 'delle Bande Nere' dei Medici**, married his kinswoman, a grand-daughter of **Lorenzo the Magnificent dei Medici**: thus continuing the Medici dynasty in Florence who became **Grand Dukes of Tuscany** (for which see Table 23), HRH's distinguished ancestors (through the **Princess of Wales**) who did so much to beautify Florence, and to whose art collections Italy and the whole world owe so much.

GISILBERT, *Count on the Meuse (in what is now Belgium), kidnapped & m. Emperor* LOTHAIR's *dau.* IRMGARD *846*

REGINAR I, *Margrave between the Meuse & Scheldt, Count of Hainault, Abbot of Echternach, mastered all Lorraine, d.915*

REGINAR II, *Count of Hainault, with his capital at Mons but his principal residence in the castle of Hornu, d. c.932*

REGINAR III *'Long-Neck', Duke of Upper Lorraine, reformed his monasteries, captured at war with Emperor* OTTO *the Great, d. in exile 973*

LAMBERT I *'the Bearded', Count of Louvain, including Brussels, 'one of the most energetic personalities of feudal Belgium', slain in battle 1015*

LAMBERT II *'the Belted', Count of Louvain, founded the greatness of the city of Brussels, d. c.1063*

HENRY II, *Count of Louvain, whose aid was invoked by* RICHILDE *of Flanders against* ROBERT *the Frisian, d.1078*

GODFREY I *'the Bearded', Duke of Lower Lorraine & Marquis of Antwerp (m.* IDA, *dau. of* ALBERT III, *Marquis of Namur), d. c.1040*

GODFREY II, *Duke of Lower Lorraine, d.1142 (his bro.* JOSCELINE *m. the* PERCY *heiress and was male line forefather of* HRH's *ancestors the* PERCY *earls of Northumberland)*

GODREY III *'the Babe', Duke of Lower Lorraine, d.1190 (m.* MARGARET, *dau. of his foe* HENRY II, *Duke of Limbourg, ancestor of* LUXEMBOURGS)

HENRY I *'the Warrior', Duke of Brabant, soldier-statesman, crusader with Richard Coeur-de-Lion against Saladin in Holy Land, d.1235*

HENRY II, *Duke of Brabant, d.1248 (his younger son* HENRY *was male line forefather of* HRH's *ancestors, the Houses of* HESSE & MOUNTBATTEN)

HENRY III *'the Peaceful', Duke of Brabant, succeeded father as a Margrave of Holy Roman Empire, d.1261*

JOHN I *'the Victorious', Duke of Brabant, killed* WALERAN, *Count of Luxembourg with his own sword in battle 1288, d. of tournament wounds 1294*

JOHN II *'the Peaceful', Duke of Brabant, knighted in Brussels by father-in-law King* EDWARD I *of England; d.1312*

JOHN III *'the Triumphant', Duke of Brabant, d.1355, last of immediate male line (cadet male line continues in* HESSE & MOUNTBATTENS)

MARGARET *of Brabant (her descendants were heirs of her sister Joan, Duchess of Lorraine, Brabant & Limbourg) d.1368; m.* LOUIS III *de Mâle, Count of Flanders (temporarily expelled from Bruges by Artevelde 1382) d.1384*

MARGARET *of Flanders, heiress of Flanders, Artois & the Franche-Comté of Burgundy, d.1405; m.* PHILIP *the Bold, Capetian Duke of Burgundy, defeated and slew Philip van Artevelde 1382; d.1404*

JOHN *the Fearless, Duke of Burgundy, assassinated at bridge of Montereau 1419; m.* MARGARET, *dau. of* ALBERT, *Count of Holland, Zealand, Hainault and Friesland (& heiress in her issue)*

PHILIP *the Good, Duke of Burgundy, founded at Bruges celebrated Order of the Golden Fleece, d.1467*

CHARLES *the Bold, Duke of Burgundy, sought imperial recognition of a Burgundian kingdom of Arles or 'Belgian Gaul', slain in battle 1477*

MARY *of Burgundy, heiress of Holland, Zealand, Friesland, Gelderland, Hainault, Brabant, Flanders, Limbourg & Luxembourg, d. fall from horse 1482; m. Emperor* MAXIMILIAN I *of Habsburg, d.1519*

Archduke PHILIP *the Fair, K. Consort of Spain, heir apparent of the Netherlands, d.1506*

ancestors of HRH *See Tables 18 & 38*

WILLIAM *the Silent, Prince of Orange, Stadtholder of the Netherlands in revolt 1572, Founder of the Dutch Republic, assassinated 1584; m.* LOUISE, *dau. of* GASPARD DE COLIGNY, *Admiral of France, leader of Huguenots, slain in massacre of St Bartholomew*

FREDERICK HENRY, *Prince of Orange, Stadtholder of United Provinces 1625, 'golden age of the republic', made peace with Spain, d.1647*

LOUISA HENRIETTA *of Orange-Nassau, d.1667; m.* FREDERICK WILLIAM, *the 'Great Elector' of Brandenburg, d.1688*

FREDERICK I, *K. in Prussia, d.1713*

ancestors of HRH   *See Table 19*

LUXEMBOURG

For HRH's LUXEMBOURG *ancestors: see Table 15*

William the Silent, Prince of Orange, founder of the Dutch republic, assassinated 1584

THE LOW COUNTRIES

THE Low Countries, now forming Benelux – the kingdoms of Belgium and the Netherlands with the grand duchy of Luxembourg – were part of the kingdom of Lotharingia (Lorraine), called after HRH's Carolingian ancestor, the **Emperor Lothair**, which was established for him by the Treaty of Verdun in 843, when the vast Frankish empire was divided among the three sons of the **Emperor Louis the Pious**, son of **Charlemagne**: Lothair's two brothers getting what became France and Germany on either side of his buffer realm. The Low Countries themselves, Lower Lorraine, were divided up under the administration of various Counts, of which the most important eventually evolved into semi-independent states under the **Dukes of Brabant**, also the **Counts of Flanders, Hainault, Holland, Gelderland, Limbourg** and **Luxembourg**, all originally ancestors of HRH.

Of these, the **Dukes of Brabant** descended from princess **Irmgard**, daughter of the **Emperor Lothair**: she was abducted by **Count Gisilbert of the Meuse** in 846 and carried off to Aquitaine, where he married her. **Count Gisilbert** was ancestor in the direct male line of **Harry 'Hotspur', Lord Percy**, KG (slain in battle 1403) and of **Prince Philip**'s maternal uncle Louis, Earl Mountbatten of Burma, KG, last Viceroy of India (assassinated by the IRA 1979): **Count Gisilbert**'s own ancestors have not yet been traced, though his traditional forefathers had been counts or dukes from time out of mind and 'perhaps there is even reason to link them to the *Ragnacharius (Reginar), King of Cambrai*, who according to Gregory of Tours was a kinsman of Clovis', and thus fifth-century Salian Frankish royalty of Woden-born sacral Merovingian stock.

HRH descends not only from the various counts of these little countries, but also from families such as **Buren, Culemborg, Bronkhorst** and **Baer** who were originally called bannerets (displaying their own banners in the field) and were themselves semi-independent of the **Counts of Zutphen** or of **Gelderland** (before it became a duchy).

Famous names abound among HRH's mediaeval

ancestors: **van der Boetzelaer** and **Heeckeren**, **Brederode** and **Schenk van Tautenburg**, **Merode** and **Lannoy**, **van Pallandt**, **Arkel** and **van Zuylen**. They held the high offices: thus **Jean, Seigneur de Lannoy**, was Stadtholder of Utrecht 1448–65, and **Wolfert VI van Borseln, Count of Grandpré**, who died in 1487, was Governor of Holland. More recent forefathers of HRH include **Charles de Croy, Prince of Chimay** (died 1527), **Charles de Ligne, Prince of Arenberg**, Governor of the Spanish Netherlands (died 1616) and **Philip Lamoral, Count of Hornes** or Horn (died 1663); not to mention the great Dutch families of **Bentinck duke of Portland** and **Keppel earl of Albemarle** who settled in England under the House of Orange.

For the **House of Luxembourg**, sprung from **Count Siegfried on the Moselle** who acquired Luxembourg in 963 and whose dynasty became Kings of Bohemia and then Holy Roman Emperors in the fourteenth and fifteenth centuries, see the section on the Czechs; and for HRH's descent through Guise from the **House of Lorraine**, see Table 13. HRH also has many lines of descent from the original **Dukes of Lower Lorraine** who had a tradition of descent from *Ida*, daughter of the Swan Knight *Lohengrin*: Lotharingian Garin or Garin of Lorraine – and the Swan often appears in the heraldry of their descendants, among whom were HRH's ancestors the **Dukes of Cleves**, who had a Swan Tower in their Swan Castle, the Schwanenburg. During the fifteenth century, the eventual heiress of the dynasty founded by **Dirk I, Count of Holland** in 922, who was probably son of the Frisian *Count Gerolf* (899), carried Holland, Zealand, Frisia and Hainault to the **Dukes of Burgundy**; who had already married the eventual heiress of the line of the **Counts of Flanders**, founded by **Count Baldwin** who had died c.879. These territories, with their great trading cities, made Burgundy the richest country in Europe, and **Duke Charles the Bold** nearly obtained imperial recognition as King of Arles or 'Belgian Gaul'. He had persuaded HRH's other ancestor, the **Emperor Frederick III**, to crown him at Trier; but his forceful attitude displeased the Habsburg emperor, who promptly fled by night, and the coronation never took place.

In the end, however, the Habsburgs themselves obtained this vast and wealthy inheritance by the marriage of **Frederick III**'s son, the **Emperor Maximilian I**, to **Duke Charles the Bold**'s daughter. Unfortunately for the Low Countries, however, the great-grandson of this marriage, Philip II, was very much the Catholic King of

Charles the Bold, Duke of Burgundy (slain in battle 1477), whose likeness to his descendant Prince Charles was recently commented on in *The Times*

Spain. Political and religious differences arose with the Dutch. Two of their principal noblemen were arrested in 1568, refused their right to be tried by their fellow Knights of the Golden Fleece and sentenced to death by order of the Council of Blood set up by the Duke of Alba, HRH's ancestral uncle, although he was himself a Knight of the Fleece. Moreover, one of these two martyrs to the Dutch cause was HRH's direct ancestor **Lamoral, Count of Egmont** (Egmond), Prince of Gavre and Stadtholder of Flanders, victor of Gravelines, and who was promptly beheaded in the square in front of the town hall at Brussels, behaving with great dignity. 'From this memorable event, which Goethe made the theme of his play *Egmont* (1788), is usually dated the beginning of the famous revolt of the Netherlands.'

The leader of this revolt was **William the Silent, Prince of Orange**, HRH's ancestor through both the **Prince and Princess of Wales**. By his skill and determination, he was the founder of the Dutch Republic. Although **William the Silent** was assassinated by a fanatic in 1584, Holland began her golden age when his son **Frederick Henry, Prince of Orange** was Stadtholder of the United Provinces, 1625–47, and peace was made at last with Spain. And when the Netherlands eventually became a kingdom, the Dutch chose the House of Orange as their royal family.

28 POLAND
Piast

MIESZKO I, *Duke of Poland 964–92 (descended from semi-legendary Prince* PIAST) *was converted to Christianity*

BOLESLAW I *the Brave, K. of Poland from 1000, d.1025, fought Germans, then Russians*

MIESZKO II, *K. of Poland 1025–34 (temporarily deposed 1031–2 by bro. Bezprim)*

CASIMIR I, *Duke of Poland 1039–58, founded two Cluniac monasteries*

WLADISLAW *Herman, Duke of Poland, poisoned 1102 (bro. of K. Boleslaw the Bold, exiled for killing Bishop of Cracow)*

BOLESLAW III *'Wry-Mouth', Duke of Poland, 1102–38, acquired Pomerania, thus access to Baltic sea*

CASIMIR II *the Just, Duke of Little Poland 1177–94, seized Cracow 1177, founded Council that led to Senate*

CONRAD, *Duke of Masovia, invaded by the Mongols 1241, allowed Teutonic Knights to settle in Prussia, d.1247*

CASIMIR, *Duke of Cujavia, which his father gave him in 1233, d.1267*

WLADISLAW I *the Short, K. of Poland 1320–33, previously Duke of Cracow, where he was crowned in the cathedral*

CASIMIR III *the Great, K. of Poland 1333–70, the 'peasants' king', 'this really great monarch', d. from a fall out hunting*

ELISABETH *of Poland (Piast princess) d.1361; m.* BOGESLAV I, *Duke of Pomerania, d.1373*

ELISABETH *of Pomerania, Empress, d.1393; m. Emperor* CHARLES IV, *K. of Bohemia, d.1378*

Emperor SIGISMUND, *K. of Hungary & Bohemia, d.1437*

ancestors of HRH   *See Table 15*

29 POLAND & LITHUANIA
Jagiellon

LUTUWER, *pagan Grand Prince of Lithuania, d.1293, whose dynasty were buried with their horses*

GEDIMIN, *Styled K. of the Lithuanians and many Ruthenians, last pagan ruler, founded Vilna, d.1341*

OLGIERD *Alexander, Grand Prince of Lithuania 1345–77, was baptised a Christian*

WLADISLAW II, *K. of Poland from 1386 (formerly* JAGIELLO, *as Grand Prince of Lithuania), d.1434 aged 83*

CASIMIR IV, *K. of Poland 1447–92, made peace with Teutonic Knights as his nominal vassals, d. of dropsy*

SIGISMUND I *the Old, K. of Poland 1506–48 (his bro. K.* WLADISLAW III *was also* HRH's *ancestor) ennobled professors*

JADWIGA *Jagiellon of Poland, d.1573; m.* JOACHIM II, *Elector of Brandenburg d.1571 (as his second wife)*

HEDWIG *of Brandenburg, d.1602; m.* JULIUS, *Duke of Brunswick-Wolfenbüttel, d.1589*

HENRY JULIUS, *Duke of Brunswick-Wolfenbüttel, d.1613*

ELISABETH *of Brunswick, d.1650; m.* JOHN PHILIP, *Duke of Saxe-Altenburg, d.1639*

ELISABETH SOPHIA *of Saxony, d.1680; m.* ERNEST I,
Duke of Saxe-Gotha, d.1675

FREDERICK I, *Duke of Saxe-Gotha, d.1691 (female
line descendant of Emperor* FERDINAND I *of
Habsburg)*

FREDERICK II, *Duke of Saxe-Gotha, d.1732*

AUGUSTA *of Saxony, Princess of Wales, d.1772; m.*
FREDERICK, *Prince of Wales, 'poor Fred, was
alive, is dead', d.1751*

GEORGE III, *K. of Great Britain, d.1820*

ancestors of HRH

POLAND & LITHUANIA

THE sacral princes of the pagan Poles descended
from the semi-legendary **Prince Piast**,
842–61, after whom their dynasty was named.
According to their chroniclers, he was father of
Prince Ziemowit, (died 892) who wrested the
great province of Chrobacyja from the Moravians,
father of **Prince Leszek IV**, 892–913 (died 921),
father of **Prince Ziemonislaw** (died 964), last
pagan prince, father of **Prince Mscislaw**, better
known as **Mieszko I, Duke of Poland** 964–92,
who married the Christian princess **Dobrawa of
Bohemia** and was himself converted to Christianity.

His son, **Boleslaw the Brave**, was made **King
of Poland** by the Emperor Otto in 1000: 'he was
primarily a warrior, whose reign, an almost unin-
terrupted warfare, resulted in the formation of a
vast kingdom extending from the Baltic to the
Carpathians, and from the Elbe to the Bug'. But
after his death, Poland was attacked – as so often
throughout her valiant history – by all her neighbours, 'and simultaneously a terrible pagan reaction
swept away the poor remnants of Christianity and
civilisation. For a time Poland proper became a
smoking wilderness, and wild beasts made their
lairs in the ruined and desecrated churches'.

King Boleslaw 'Wry-Mouth', so named
because his mouth was twisted from an old wound
received in battle, restored Polish power, conquered the heathen Pomeranians and forcibly converted them to Christianity, thereby also regaining
access to the Baltic sea. Unfortunately, when he
died in 1138, **Boleslaw** divided his realm among
four of his sons, a nominal supremacy resting with
whichever ducal branch held Cracow.

When the Mongols invaded Europe in 1241 – and
indeed would probably have reached the Atlantic,
just as they had already reached the Pacific, had
news not reached them of their Great Khan's death
in far-off Karakorum a year's ride away for the
fastest couriers – they soon entered Poland and
burnt Cracow to ashes. Every day still, a trumpeter

Cup given to the cathedral of Plock by HRH's Polish
ancestor Conrad I, Duke of Masovia (d.1247)

Seal of Casimir the Great, King of Poland
1333–70, the peasants' king

sounds the alarm from the tower of Cracow cathedral: but the trumpet call is always broken off stifled at the moment when a Mongol arrow struck the original look-out in mid-call. One of the principal **Piast** dynasts then was HRH's worried forefather **Henry the Pious, Duke of Silesia**, who gathered the northern princes, together with the Teutonic Knights, to meet the Mongols in battle at Liegnitz (now called Legnica). Totally defeated, and his horse having dropped from exhaustion in the flight, **Duke Henry** tried to escape running on foot, hampered by his heavy armour, but the Mongol horsemen soon caught up with him and rode off in triumph with his severed head on a spear. His widow, the Czech princess **Anne of Bohemia**, only identified his headless, mangled, naked corpse because **Duke Henry** had six toes on his left foot. Meanwhile, the victorious Mongols filled nine large sacks with a single ear from each of their slain opponents.

Poland was not re-established as a single entity until **Wladislaw the Short** reunited the realm in 1320, following this up by his smashing victory over the iron-clad Teutonic Knights at Plowce. His son, **King Casimir the Great**, was 'Poland's first great statesman in the modern sense of the word', who protected the peasants and the townsfolk, reformed the administration, encouraged trade, and whose 'few wars were waged entirely for profit, not for glory'. He was the last of the **Piast** sovereigns; and sixteen years after his death, the first of the **Jagiellon** dynasty became **King of Poland.**

This royal house came from Lithuania. Their ancestor, the **Grand Prince Lutuwer**, who died in 1293, belonged to a pagan dynasty who were still buried with their horses. **Lutuwer**'s son, the famous **Gedimin**, styled **'King of the Lithuanians and of many Ruthenians'**, tolerated Catholic and Orthodox Christians alike, but remained a heathen himself, burning amber in sacrifice before a green snake, maintaining the sacred oak groves, and when he founded the castle at Vilna, built a temple to preserve the sacred fire. He died in 1341 of a wound received at the siege of Wiclowa. But Vilna remained the capital of the Lithuanian grand princes, and his son, the diplomatic **Grand Prince Olgierd**, became a Christian. It was **Olgierd**'s son, the **Grand Prince Jagiello**, who in 1386 was crowned **King of Poland** under the throne-name of **King Wladislaw II**, in the cathedral of Cracow.

King Wladislaw II Jagiello reigned for forty-nine years, making Poland a great power before his death at the age of eighty-three. His son, **King Casimir IV Jagiellon**, was an equally great statesmen, under whose own son, **King Sigismund the Old** (died 1548), the duchy of Masovia with its now famous capital of Warsaw was reincorporated in the turbulent Kingdom of Poland. Thus HRH is a direct descendant of the greatest kings of the two great native dynasties of the Poles and Lithuanians: the **Piasts** and the **Jagiellons.**

HENRY, *Count of Portugal 1093–1112 (of Burgundian branch of Royal House of France); m.* TERESA, *natural dau. of* ALFONSO VI, *K. of Leon, who gave her Portugal for dowry*

AFFONSO *Henriques, K. of Portugal from 1139 (recognised 1143), founder of the nation, d. 1185*

SANCHO I, *K. of Portugal 1185–1211, o Povoador 'the maker of towns', retired to die in a monastery*

AFFONSO II *the Fat, K. of Portugal 1211–23, only let his sisters have their estates if they became nuns*

AFFONSO III, *K. of Portugal 1245–79 (dethroned bro. K. Sancho II), made Lisbon his capital*

DINIZ, *K. of Portugal 1279–1325, the 'farmer king', poet, patron of music & literature, founded first University*

AFFONSO IV *the Brave, K. of Portugal 1325–57, gallant crusader against Moors of Granada*

PEDRO *the Severe, K. of Portugal 1357–67, took exemplary vengeance on murderers of his secret second wife*

JOHN I *the Great, K. of Portugal 1383–1433 (natural son: founded House of Aviz) 'father of his country', ally of England*

AFFONSO, *Duke of Braganza (natural bro. of K.* DUARTE, *1433–8) d.1461; m.* BEATRICE, *dau. of* NUNO *Alvarez Pereira, Count of Ourem,* THE HOLY CONSTABLE, *victor of Aljubarrota*

ISABEL *of Braganza, d.1465; m. her half-uncle Infante Dom* JOHN *of Portugal (bro. of K.* DUARTE *& Henry the Navigator)*

ISABEL *of Portugal, d.1496; m.* JOHN II, *K. of Castile (son of* FERNANDO I, *K. of Castile, by* ELEANOR, *dau. of* SANCHO, *Count of Albuquerque)*

FERDINAND, *K. of Castile & Aragon (with his wife Queen* ISABELLA, *sent Columbus to America)*

ancestors of HRH *See Table 38*

PORTUGAL

Portugal came into being when it was given as a fief fo HRH's ancestor **Count Henry of Burgundy** as dowry when the count married **King Alfonso VI of Leon**'s natural daughter **Teresa**, a lady of strong character who afterwards acted as Guardian of Portugal both when her husband was away on crusade in Palestine and, after his death, for their infant son, **Dom Affonso Henriques**. The **Count Henry** himself was younger son of **Henry**, son of **Robert, Duke of Burgundy**, in turn son of **Robert, King of France** 996–1031, of the great **Capetian** dynasty for which see the section on France. **Countess Teresa** was of the old Visigothic stock, descended through her mother from **Bermudo I, King of Asturias** 788–91, himself grandson of **Pedro, Duke in Calabria**, and which had held out against the Arab conquerors of most of the Iberian peninsula after 714 and had been gradually reconquering their lost territory over the centuries.

Count Affonso Henriques made himself the first independent **King of Portugal**. 'One of the warrior heroes of mediaeval romance; his exploits were sung by troubadours throughout south-western Europe, and even in Africa "ibn Errik" – the son of Henry – was known and feared.' In 1139 he won a signal victory over the combined forces of the Moors at Ourique, and tradition has it that after this battle the Portuguese soldiers raised **Dom Affonso** on their shields and hailed him as king in the old Visigothic manner: though it was some time before Castile & Leon recognised Portugal as an independent kingdom.

Although suffering from an old wound, **King Affonso I** won many more victories over the Moors, and in 1147 captured Lisbon itself. His son, **King Sancho I**, carried on the good work and built many towns during a warlike life, before retiring to die in peace in the monastery at Alcobaço. In the next reign, **King Affonso the Fat** instituted the

Tomb at Batalha of King John the Great (1383–1443) founder of the House of Aviz and his wife Philippa, daughter of John of Gaunt, Duke of Lancaster

first Portuguese *cortes* or parliament of bishops, abbots and nobles. His elder son was deposed after an unpopular marriage, in favour of the next son, who became **King Affonso III** and whose own marriage to **Beatrice**, natural daughter of **King Alfonso IX of Castile** by **Donna Maria Guillen de Guzman**, a descendant of the famous **Counts of Lara**, may well have brought some of the most distinguished Arab blood in Spain (that of the *Ummayad caliphs of Cordoba* and the *Abbadid emirs of Seville*) into HRH's ancestry. Under **King Affonso III** the monarchy secured the support of the towns and the military orders, agreed that taxation would require the agreement of the *cortes*, made Lisbon the capital, and got Castilian recognition that the great province of Algarve should form part of independent Portugal.

His son, **Dom Diniz**, the 'Farmer King', inherited the talents of this remarkable family: founding agricultural schools as well as Portugal's first university, which eventually moved from Lisbon to Coimbra, **King Diniz** 'was also a poet of exquisite taste, developing the Portuguese dialect into a beautiful and flexible language. The king went

further: as he grew older, he threw off the trammels of Provençal forms, and perceiving the beauty of his people's lyrics, he wrote some graceful "pastorellas" inspired by their influence,' in which he was 'the forerunner of the great pastoral school' and indeed 'the founder of Portuguese literature'.

Dom Diniz's queen, who was afterwards canonised as **St Isabel**, prevented a pitched battle between her husband and his rebellious eldest son, later **King Affonso the Brave**, by riding in person between the rival armies. In 1355, this **King Affonso** was unhappily privy to the ghastly murder, despite her tears and pleading for mercy, of his son and heir **Dom Pedro**'s secret second wife, the beautiful and adorable **Donna Ines de Castro**, an illegitimate but noble lady, by three courtiers, one of whom was the Lord Chamberlain himself and another the powerful noble **Dom Diego Lopes Pacheco**. After his accession, **King Pedro the Severe** had her cruel murderers extradited from Castile, whither they had fled, and two of them were publicly tortured to death in his presence: but **Dom Diego Pacheco** escaped to England through the assistance of a beggar to whom he had once done a kindness. Then the new king had the body of his beloved **Ines de Castro** disinterred at Coimbra, and taken to Alcobaça, where it was solemnly enthroned and crowned – according to one account, while the assembled nobles of Portugal kissed 'the withered hand of the corpse' – before being sealed in a marble sarcophagus, placed opposite his own, foot to foot, so that at the Resurrection they would rise up facing each other again. But the brutal Napoleonic soldiery forced open her tomb in 1810, taking the yellow hair from her broken skeleton for a souvenir in their search for jewels. By coincidence, **Prince Charles** descends from **Ines de Castro**, and the **Princess of Wales** from her murderer **Pacheco**: so HRH descends from both.

A generation later, when it was feared that Portugal might be united with Castile, **King Pedro**'s natural son **Dom John**, Grand Master of the Knights of Aviz, was made **Defender of the Realm** by a popular uprising led by the aristocracy, and thus founded the famous **House of Aviz**. When a great Castilian army then invaded the country, the *cortes* unanimously elected **Dom John** to be **King of Portugal**; and with the assistance of his heroic general, the **Holy Constable**, he inflicted a decisive defeat on the Spaniards in 1385 at Aljubarrota, which secured the independence of Portugal. **King John the Great**, as he was now called, erected the splendid convent of Batalha on the battlefield, named like our own Battle Abbey on the field of Hastings. **King John** had been assisted by English archers; and in 1386, by the Treaty of Windsor, he made the famous Alliance between Portugal and England which lasted into the twentieth century. Later, he married **John of Gaunt**'s daughter and their son, afterwards **King Duarte** and an ancestor of HRH, was called after his maternal uncle Edward the Black Prince.

HRH had numerous ancestors among the higher aristocracy of Portugal during those formative centuries. Among them, for instance, was **Sancho, Count of Albuquerque**. But the **Holy Constable**, whose full name was **Dom Nuno Alvarez Pereira, Count of Ourem & Constable of Portugal**, was unquestionably HRH's most distin-

HRH's ancestor Dom Nuno Alvarez Pereira, the 'Holy Constable' of Portugal, victor of the battle of Aljubarrota (1385)

guished Portuguese ancestor apart from its greatest kings: HRH having several lines of descent from the **Holy Constable**'s daughter **Beatrice** and her husband **Affonso, Duke of Braganza**, founder of the later Royal House of Braganza and natural brother both of **Duarte, King of Portugal** and also of the celebrated Infante Dom Henry the Navigator, who so wisely organised the explorations down the coast of Africa that laid the foundations of Portugal's wealth and future world-wide empire.

BOGDAN I, *Voivode of Moldavia 1349–65, expelled Tatars from Moldavian lowlands*

LAȚCO, *Voivode of Moldavia 1370–2*

ANASTASIA *of Moldavia, m. Voivode* ROMAN I *1392–3, son of* COSTEA I *Mușat, Voivode of Moldavia 1387–9*

ALEXANDER I *the Good, also called the Old, Voivode of Moldavia 1401–33*

BOGDAN II, *Voivode of Moldavia 1449–51*

STEPHEN III *the Great, Voivode of Moldavia 1456–1504, defeated Turkish & Polish invaders*

PETER III *Rareș the Poisoner, Voivode of Moldavia d.1546 (natural son) forced to submit to Turks*

CHIAÏNA *Despina Regina of Moldavia (sister of Voivodes Stephen VI d.1552 & John IV d.1583); m.* MIRCEA *the Shepherd, Voivode of Valachia d.1560*

STANCA *Basarab of Valachia*

ancestors of HRH *(see below 32)*

BASARAB, *Voivode of Valachia (probably son of* TOKTEMIR, *gt-grandson of* JUCHI, *son of* GENGHIS KHAN)

ALEXANDER I, *Voivode of Valachia, d.1360*

RADU I *the Black, Voivode of Valachia 1372–83 (bro. of Voivode Vlad I, 1360–72)*

MIRCEA I *the Old, Voivode of Valachia & Despot of the Dobrudja, d.1418, obliged to accept Turkish suzerainty*

VLAD II *Dracul 'the Dragon', Voivode of Valachia, 1430–46, granted Order of the Dragon by Emperor* SIGISMUND

Voivode VLAD IV *the Monk, d.1507 (natural bro. of Voivode Vlad Dracula the Impaler, who was slain 1476)*

RADU IV *the Great, Voivode of Valachia 1495–1508, 'laid down the first ecclesiastical organisation in Valachia'*

MIRCEA III *the Shepherd, Voivode of Valachia, d.1560 (m.* CHIAÏNA, *dau. of Peter III of Moldavia, see above)*

STANCA *Basarab of Valachia (sister of Voivodes Alexander II d.1577; & Peter II, who also ruled Moldavia), m.* JOHN *Norocza, Logofat of Pitești, Great Chancellor of Valachia 1589, d. a refugee in Transylvania 1599*

ZAMPHIRA *Logofat de Szászebes, d. c.1602; m.* PETER *Rácz de Galgó, Ambassador of Transylvania & Poland to Sublime Porte (Turkey) 1571–83*

ADAM *Rácz de Galgó, living 1609, Transylvanian noble*

PETER *Rácz de Galgó, living 1672, Transylvanian noble*

CHRISTINA *Rácz de Galgó, m.* NICHOLAS *Kuún de Osdola*

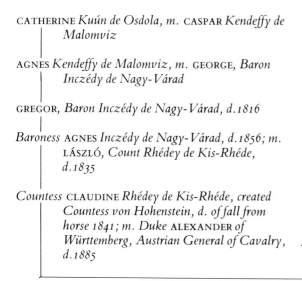

CATHERINE *Kuún de Osdola, m.* CASPAR *Kendeffy de Malomviz*

AGNES *Kendeffy de Malomviz, m.* GEORGE, *Baron Inczédy de Nagy-Várad*

GREGOR, *Baron Inczédy de Nagy-Várad, d.1816*

Baroness AGNES *Inczédy de Nagy-Várad, d.1856; m.* LÁSZLÓ, *Count Rhédey de Kis-Rhéde, d.1835*

Countess CLAUDINE *Rhédey de Kis-Rhéde, created Countess von Hohenstein, d. of fall from horse 1841; m. Duke* ALEXANDER *of Württemberg, Austrian General of Cavalry, d.1885*

FRANCIS, *Duke of Teck,* GCB, *d.1900 (m. Princess* MARY ADELAIDE *of Cambridge)*

Princess MARY *of Teck, Queen Consort of Great Britain, d.1953; m.* GEORGE V, *K. of Great Britain, Emperor of India, d.1936*

GEORGE VI, *K. of Great Britain, last Emperor of India, d.1952*

Queen ELIZABETH II, *Head of the Commonwealth, b.1926; m. Prince* PHILIP, *Duke of Edinburgh, b.1921*

Prince CHARLES, *Prince of Wales, b.1948*

HRH

ROMANIA

IN classical times, much of what is now Romania was the Roman province of Dacia, hence the proud name 'Romania' and the Latin character and vocabulary of much of its language. Later, the Romanian-speaking peoples were divided into the principalities of Valachia and Moldavia, under their own voivodes or princes, and that of Transylvania which was ruled by chosen Magyar voivodes under the kingdom of Hungary. All three were only united into the present country of Romania in comparatively modern times.

For HRH's ancestors who were Voivodes of Transylvania, see under Hungary (p. 85), as the principality of Transylvania formed a major part of the kingdom of Hungary from 1004 until after the First World War, except for a brief period of independence from 1538 to 1691 under Princes who were related to HRH.

But the great historic nucleus of Romania was the twin principalities of Valachia and Moldavia, formed early in the fourteenth century, whose rulers were usually styled 'Voivode' although the Romanian title is more correctly 'Domnul'. In the previous century, the whole country (together with Poland and Hungary) had been overrun by the Mongols, whose southern forces had ravaged Valachia and Moldavia before forcing the Carpathian mountain passes into Transylvania in 1241, and the Khans of the Golden Horde were still the suzerains of the Lithuanian and Russian princes, Valachia's neighbours. There seems no reason, therefore, to doubt that '**Thocomerius**', father of **Basarab the Great, Prince of Valachia** 1310–38, was one of the two contemporary Tatar princes both named

Toktemir in that area, both great-grandsons of prince **Juchi**, first **Khan of the Golden Horde** (died 1224), predeceasing eldest son of **Genghis Khan**, the Mongol 'Emperor of All Men'. **Juchi**'s descendants, as Khans of the Golden Horde, were suzerains from the mouth of the Danube to the easternmost limits of Siberia.

Prince Basarab the Great of Valachia inflicted a crushing defeat on the Hungarians in 1330, and the prowess of **Prince Mircea the Old** is still celebrated in Romanian national folk-songs. However, he allied himself with his former foe **King Sigismund of Hungary** under the supreme command of **John the Fearless, Count of Nevers** (afterwards **Duke of Burgundy**) in a great crusade against the Turks which, owing to **Prince Mircea**'s wise battle-plan being ignored, was totally defeated at Nicopolis in 1396.

Today, perhaps the most famous of HRH's Romanian relations is Prince Vlad Dracula 'the Impaler', an ancestral uncle who took the surname of Dracula because his father **Prince Vlad Dracul** was proud to be a Knight of the Dragon, an order founded by the same **Sigismund**, now **Holy Roman Emperor**, to combat heretics and infidels, 'dracul' being the Romanian word for 'dragon'. Because Bram Stoker took his name of Dracula for the anti-hero of his famous novel, some people suppose Prince Vlad to have been a vampire. But he was not: his Romanian nickname 'Tepeş' means Impaler. He had picked up the thrill of seeing people writhing on stakes while a hostage in Istanbul, and even when a state prisoner in Hungary used to catch and impale mice in his cell.

Fifteenth-century woodcut of HRH's ancestral uncle Vlad Dracula 'the Impaler', slain 1476

We learn of Prince Vlad Dracula that 'usually the stakes were carefully rounded at the end and bathed in oil so that the entrails of the victim should not be pierced by a wound too fatal when the victim's legs were stretched wide apart and two horses (one attached to each leg) were sent cantering in different directions, while attendants held the stake and body firmly in place', but his prisoners were often impaled with sharpened stakes through other parts of the body. The minimum number of his victims has been estimated at 40,000 out of a population of less than half a million. But he turned it to good account in a crisis. When Sultan Mehmet the Conqueror approached Vlad Dracula's capital in 1462, the gates of the city were left open, but 'a frightful scene greeted the sultan in a narrow gorge one mile long, just outside the city. There, the sultan's eyes caught sight of the remains of over 20,000 mangled, rotting men, women and children.' The horrified sultan ordered a deep ditch to be dug around the whole Turkish encampment that very night, and withdrew the following day.

Dracula's half-brother, who disapproved of him and opposed him politically at great personal risk, was HRH's ancestor **Vlad IV, Voivode of Valachia** 1480–94, a ruler of rather less ferocious character, and abdicated to become a monk, taking the religious name of **Pahonie**. Meanwhile, HRH's Moldavian ancestors had also had trouble with the Turks, and in 1474 **Stephen the Great, Voivode of Moldavia** had gained a great victory at Rahova over the Sultan Mehmet himself (the conqueror of Constantinople), over 400 Turkish banners being captured and four pashas among the slain. HRH has therefore both Valachian and Moldavian princely blood of the utmost distinction in Romanian history.

RURIK *(Hroerekr), Woden-born K. of Lethra (gt. grandson of* RURIK, *Skiöldung prince at Lethra), m.* AUD, *dau. of* IVAR *Wide-Fathom of Skane, K. of Uppsala in Sweden & Lethra in Denmark*

HARALD *Hilditönn, K. of Lethra in Sjealland (Denmark), slain in sea battle at Bravik 770*

HALFDAN, *Margrave of Frisia c.782 when exiled to the Frankish empire*

RURIK, *invited by the Varangians to Rus to become first Prince of Novgorod in 862, d.875*

IGOR, *Grand Prince of Kiev (possibly grandson), slain raiding Derevlians for tribute 945; m.* OLGA, *Regent of Russia 945–64, fiercely avenged her husband, d.969*

SVIATOSLAV I, *Grand Prince of Kiev, killed by Pechenegs, who made his skull a drinking cup, 972*

St VLADIMIR I, *Grand Prince of Kiev, a great conqueror, converted from paganism, Christianised all Russia, d.1015*

YAROSLAV I *the Wise, Grand Prince of Kiev, 'the last grand prince who upheld vigorously the old system', d.1054*

VSEVOLOD I, *Grand Prince of Kiev, 'loved justice, aided the poor, abstained from drunkenness', d.1093*

VLADIMIR II *Monomakh, Grand Prince of Kiev, 'pious, judicious and intelligent', d.1125*

YURI I *Dolgoruky (Long-Hands), Prince of Suzdal, founder of Moscow in 1147, d.1157*

VSEVOLOD III, *Grand Prince of Vladimir, d.1212; m. the Osset princess* MARY *(the Ossets or Alans were Sarmatians sprung from Scyths & Amazons)*

YAROSLAV II, *Grand Prince of Suzdal & Vladimir, poisoned at Karakorum by Great Khan's mother 1246*

YAROSLAV III *Athanase, Grand Prince of Novgorod d.1271 (bro. of epic hero St Alexander Nevsky)*

MICHAEL II *the Saint, Grand Prince of Tver & Vladimir, executed by Tatars 1319; m.* ANNA *of Rostov (gt.-gt.-granddau. of Grand Prince St* MICHAEL, *martyred by Mongols 1246)*

ALEXANDER II, *Grand Prince of Tver & Vladimir, killed in camp of Tatar Khan 1339; m.* ANASTASIA, *dau. of Rurikid* YURI *Lwow, K. of Galicz (Galicia) 1301–8*

Princess N. ALEXANDROVNA *of Tver, d. after 1371; m.* SVIATOSLAV, *Grand Prince of Smolensk, killed at battle of Vekhra 1386*

Princess AGRIPPINA *of Smolensk, d. after 1401; m.* IVAN *Holczanski, Grand Duke of Russia 1379–1401*

ANDREI IVANOVICH *Holczanski, Prince of Kiev, d. by 1418*

Princess SOPHIA ANDREIEVNA *Holczanskaya, heiress of Kiev, d. 1461; m.* VLADISLAS V *Jagiello, K. of Poland d.1434*

▲ CASIMIR IV *Jagiellon, K. of Poland 1492*

ancestors of HRH   *See Table 39*

ROMAN *Yurievich, Russian boyar (noble) d.1543*

NIKITA *Romanov, Russian boyar d.1586 (bro. of Czarina Anastasia, wife of Czar Ivan IV)*

THEODORE, *Patriarch of Moscow as the metropolitan* PHILARET, *d.1633*

MICHAEL III, *Czar of Russia 1613–45, founder of Romanov dynasty*

ALEXIS I, *Czar of Russia, took Cossacks of Ukraine under his protection, d.1676*

PETER *the Great, Emperor of Russia, modernised Russia & made St Petersburg the capital, d.1725*

Grand Duchess ANNA *Petrovna of Russia d.1728; m.* CHARLES FREDERICK, *Duke of Holstein-Gottorp (of Danish royal line) d.1739*

PETER III, *Emperor of Russia, dethroned & strangled by his wife's supporters 1762; m. Empress* CATHERINE *the Great (*SOPHIE *of Anhalt, female-line descendant of epic hero Prince* IGOR*)*

PAUL I, *Emperor of Russia, inherited his father's mental eccentricities, cut down & strangled by his officers 1801*

NICHOLAS I, *Emperor of Russia, the 'Iron Czar', at war with Britain, France & Turkey in the Crimea, d.1855*

Grand Duke CONSTANTINE *of Russia, d.1892 (bro. of Alexander II, Emperor of Russia, assassinated 1881)*

Grand Duchess OLGA *of Russia, Queen of Greece, d.1926; m.* GEORGE I, *K. of the Hellenes (Prince William of Denmark) assassinated 1913*

Prince ANDREW *of Greece and Denmark, d.1944*

Prince PHILIP, *Duke of Edinburgh, b.1921*

Prince CHARLES, *Prince of Wales, b.1948*

HRH

HRH's ancestral uncle, the epic hero St Alexander Nevsky, Grand Prince of Vladimir (1220–63) who defeated the heavily-armoured Teutonic Knights when the ice gave way on frozen Lake Peipus

RUSSIA

RUSSIA took its name from the land of Rus, possibly a Finnish word for Scandinavia, whence Vikings and Norse traders sailed up the Dnieper and exacted tribute and exchanged goods with the Slavs and Finns who lived in the forests round Lake Ilmen. These Varangians, as the Scandinavians were called, used the rivers for waterways and, passing up the Dnieper and down the southern rivers to the Black Sea, eventually reached Constantinople, where they provided the famous Varangian Guard to the **Byzantine emperors**. In 862 the Slavs, quarrelling among themselves and in need of protection, asked the warlike Varangians to send for sacral royalty out of Scandinavia to reign over them. Accordingly the aged **Prince Rurik** arrived and founded the dynasty that reigned among what became the Russians for the next seven centuries.

At this time, the **Aesir** (see p. 116) were the principal sacred Scandinavian royal house on the Baltic, and modern scholars believe **Prince Rurik** to have belonged to the branch sprung from the first marriage of **King Ivar Wide-fathom**'s daughter **Aud**: to the Woden-born Skiöldung *King Rurik of Lethra* (Hroerekr Slaungvanbaugi), in whose semi-historic ancestry the almost unique royal name 'Rurik' recurs with his traditional great-grandfather *Rurik* (Hroerekr Knavggvanbaugi), son of *Ingiald, King of Lethra* in the seventh century. **Prince Rurik**'s capital was established at Novgorod, the 'new city': and from the Old Norse 'kn' root in their word for king, 'konung', meaning 'son of the (sacral royal) kindred', developed the Russian word 'kniaz' for prince, originally applied especially to the **House of Rurik**.

The princes of the **House of Rurik** established city states on the rivers throughout what became Russia, setting up independent principalities in Tver and Vladimir-Suzdal, Smolensk, Polotsk, Chernigov, Murom-Riazan, Novgorod-Seversk, Pereyaslavl, Turov, Volynsk and Galicz: for an understanding of which see *The Times Atlas of World History*, pp. 114–15. The **Rurikids** practised true primogeniture, giving the best cities to the eldest born princes, who moved from city to city as they grew older, whether brothers or cousins: and through inter-marriage among them HRH's forefathers ruled in turn over all these principalities. The head of the family at first was the Grand Prince of Kiev, 'mother of Russian cities', but later the title of Grand Prince was assumed by the most powerful

Rurikid without necessarily moving to Kiev. Within each city, local rule was fairly democratic – forerunner of the 'Soviets' – as the prince was only their protector as war-leader and sacred arbiter of the divine customary laws: there was a popular saying 'If the prince is bad, into the mud with him!'

Each **Rurikid** prince had a 'corps d'élite' called his 'druzhina' composed of noble young warriors, comparable to the Norse 'hird'; and the **Grand Prince Sviatoslav** observed: 'How can I become a Christian? My druzhina would laugh at me.' But his son, **St Vladimir**, who as a pagan had offered up human sacrifices, became a vigorous convert in 988, and with him all his people. However, **St Vladimir** had not been the sort of wooer to turn the other cheek. In 980 he fell in love with **Ragnild**, daughter of **Ragnvald, Prince of Polotsk**, but was rejected by the haughty princess because his mother **Malushka** had only been **Prince Sviatoslav**'s 'bondswoman', an attractive slave girl. **St Vladimir**, not yet a Christian, promptly conquered Polotsk, slew **Prince Ragnvald**, and took **Ragnild** for his wife by force: had the marriage not been consummated with the future saint's customary vigour, HRH could never have been born.

Indeed, these Russian princes had to be tough to be strong enough to do good. The **Grand Prince Vladimir Monomakh** married twice, HRH descending from both wives: the first was **Gytha**, daughter of the Anglo-Saxon **King Harold** killed at Hastings in 1066; and the second, daughter of **Aëpa, Khan of the Kumans** in the Asiatic steppes, was mother of **Prince Yuri Dolgoruky** who founded Moscow. Now, **Vladimir Monomakh**'s testament is revealing: 'Pass no man without a greeting; give him a kindly word. Love your wives, but grant them no power over you ... At Chernigov, I even bound wild horses with my bare hands or captured them with the lasso. Two bisons tossed me and my horse on their horns, a stag once gored me, one elk stamped upon me, while another gored me, a boar once tore my sword from my thigh, a bear on one occasion bit my kneecap, and another wild beast jumped on my flank and threw my horse with me ... I often fell from my horse, fractured my skull twice ... In war and at the hunt, by night and by day, I did whatever my servant had to do, and gave myself no rest ... I did not allow the mighty to distress the common peasant or the poverty-stricken widow.' Such were the views of a mediaeval 'Little Father' of the Russian people,

Review of the Chevalier Guards showing HRH's three ancestors Czar Nicholas I and the Czarina Alexandra Feodorovna (sister of the German Emperor William I) being saluted by Prince Alexander of Hesse and the Rhine

ancestor of HRH.

Many of HRH's forefathers had a wretched time in the struggle for survival during the period of the Tatar – more correctly Mongol – conquests and the paramountcy of the Golden Horde from the thirteenth to the fifteenth centuries. Just as the Varangians had come water-borne from the Baltic, the Mongol cavalry used the frozen rivers as roads. Thus **Yuri, Prince of Riazan** and his mother **Agrafene of Smolensk** were slaughtered when the Mongols took Riazan after a brave defence in 1237: 'Some of his people were shot in the streets or flayed alive, others were impaled and left to die in the burning buildings.' **Yuri**'s grandson **Roman,**

Prince of Riazan, was later executed by order of the Tatar khan in 1270, and the fate of several **Grand Princes of Vladimir-Suzdal** can be learnt from the attached Table 33. **Vassilko, Prince of Rostov**, fared no better on the banks of the Siti; and his father-in-law **St Michael, Grand Prince of Chernigov** rode all the way to the Great Khan's capital at Karakorum in Mongolia, over a year's journey, only to be made to walk between two fires to avert evil intent, but then executed for refusing to kneel before a statue of **Genghis Khan**.

As the Mongol suzerainty gradually declined, that of the Rurikid princes of Moscow, who had temporised with the Tatar khans, expanded. It must be remembered that the mother of Ivan the Terrible (who was a distant cousin of HRH) was a princess of the House of **Genghis Khan**. So the Muscovite grand dukes inherited the Mongol belief in a divine mission from the Eternal Blue Heaven to

Emperor Peter the Great (1689–1725)

Empress Catherine the Great (1762–96)

rule the world: and, proclaiming themselves Czars (i.e. Caesars), they rapidly pushed eastwards back along the Siberian routes established by the Mongol empire. In much of Asia, this imperial expansion was accomplished by the new dynasty established in Moscow by HRH's ancestor **Czar Michael III** in 1613: the **Romanovs**.

Of these, the most remarkable was undoubtedly **Peter the Great**, whose mother belonged to the great Russian house of **Naryshkin**, and who as a young Czar travelled incognito throughout Europe as the sailorman 'Peter Mikhailoff', learning gunnery in Prussia, anatomy and engraving in Holland, ship-building at Deptford in England, and navigation in Venice. On his return he shaved their Oriental beards off the noble boyars with his own hand, and made them adopt Western costume and ways. He conquered from Sweden the hegemony of the Baltic, where he built his new capital of St Petersburg to replace inland Moscow. In what he saw as the interests of Russia, he even treacherously decoyed home his only son, an over-gentle scholarly youth who had fled abroad, and had him given repeated floggings with a knout so that he died in agony. But the modernisation of Russia was secured.

A worthy successor to **Peter I** was his grandson's widow, **Empress Catherine II the Great**. Since she didn't wish her son **Paul** to believe she had connived at the strangling of his father, **Peter III**, she allowed it to be implied that his true father was a certain count: but no genealogical scholar of repute believes this, as when he grew up **Paul** resembled **Peter III** in so many remarkable ways, not just in physical likeness but in particular mental eccentricities. Moreover, the **Emperor Paul** himself was not deceived: after his mother's death in 1796

he had his father **Peter III**'s corpse exhumed and ceremonially re-interred, thus obliging his courtiers to do obeisance to it and making one of the assassins carry the crown – just as his direct forefather **King Peter of Portugal** had done with the exhumed and enthroned corpse of his murdered second wife **Inez de Castro** four centuries before.

However, so far as I know no historian has yet noticed that **Catherine the Great** herself introduced **Rurikid** blood into the **Romanov** dynasty, and the most romantic **Rurikid** blood at that. For she was directly descended (as therefore is HRH too) through the **Princes of Anhalt** and **King Vladislav IV of Poland** from Russia's classic hero **Prince Igor** of Novgorod-Seversky, whose adventures against the heathen Polovtsi in 1185 are told in the *Tale of Igor*, the oldest of Russian mediaeval epics.

Everybody knows the more modern tale of **Catherine the Great**'s famous voyage by river to the South in 1787, organised by her brilliant and gigantic former lover Prince Potemkin after the conquest of the Crimea on the Black Sea; when the prince is said to have had moveable villages manned by prosperous-looking peasantry shifted and re-erected along the river banks throughout the journey. But there's no doubt that Russia owed much to **Catherine**'s wise and enlightened rule.

Her grandson, the **Emperor Nicholas I**, was a martinet under whom the Russian empire was considerably extended and consolidated in Asia; but who came up against a combination of England, France and Turkey in the Crimean War, when perhaps we 'backed the wrong horse in the Eastern Question'. Today, of the Sovereigns of the then contestants, the **Prince of Wales**, and thus HRH, is equally descended from **Queen Victoria** and **Czar Nicholas I**.

INGIALD *'Ill-Ruler', K. of Uppsala in Sweden, last of Frey-born pagan sacral 'Peace-Kings', with human sacrifice in own family*

OLAF *'Tree-Hewer', K. of Vermaland in Norway, sacrificed by own people during famine, c.710*

HALFDAN *'White-Leg', K. of the Upplanders in Norway, conquered Raumariké, founded pagan temple at Skiringssal, 8th century*

EYSTEIN *'the Fart', K. in Raumariké, 8th century (m. HILD, dau. of ERIC Agnar's-son, K. in Vestfold)*

HALFDAN *'the Stingy', K. in Vestfold, 8th century, generous with gold but mean with rations*

GODFREY *'the Proud', K. in Vestfold & Raumariké, killed 810 (his bro. IVARR was ancestor of Dukes of Normandy & Jarls of Orkney)*

HALFDAN *'the Black', K. in Agdir, Vestfold &c., drowned c.863 (his bro. K. OLAF Geirstadr-Alf probably ancestor of Kings of Dublin & Mann)*

HARALD *'Fair-Hair' (Thick Hair), first Over-King of all Norway, conquered the separate fjord kingdoms, d.934*

SIGURD *'the Great', K. of Trondhjem, d. c.937 (bro. of Eric 'Blood-Axe', Over-King of Norway, later K. at York, killed 954)*

King HALFDAN *(whose cousin K. Olaf converted Norway to Christianity, forcing sacred snakes down throats of pagans who disagreed)*

SIGURD *Syr, K. in Ringeriké, d.1018*

HARALD *Haardrade ('Hard Counsel'), K. of Norway, killed in battle with Anglo-Saxon K. HAROLD at Stamford Bridge 1066*

OLAF III *'the Quiet', K. of Norway, founded city of Bergen, d.1093*

MAGNUS III *'Barefoot', K. of Norway & Dublin, undertook three campaigns in Hebrides, killed in Ireland 1103*

SIGURD I *'the Crusader', K. of Norway, previously K. of Orkney, Mann & the Isles, sacked Sidon in Palestine, d. mad 1130*

KRISTIN *(Christina), Queen of Norway, d.1178; m. SIGURD II 'Mouth', K. of Norway, murdered 1155 (son of HARALD Gille, K. of Norway, slain 1136)*

CECILIA *of Norway (half-sister of Hakon II Herdebred, K. of Norway 1161–2); m. Jarl BAARD Guttorm's-son, killed in battle 1194 (gt-grandson of Anglo-Saxon Earl TOSTIG, slain 1066)*

Jarl SKULE, *made first Norwegian duke in 1237, killed by the 'Birchlegs' 1240*

MARGARET *Skule's-daughter, Queen of Norway, d.1270; m. HAKON IV 'the Old', K. of Norway, defeated by Scots at Largs, d.1263 (natural son of K. Hakon III, murdered 1204)*

MAGNUS VI *'Law-Mender', K. of Norway, revised old heathen laws & repealed 'wergild', d.1280*

HAKON V *Haleggr, K. of Norway, reduced power of aristocracy, d.1319 (his bro. K. Eric was claimant to Scottish throne)*

INGEBORG *of Norway, Duchess of Södermanland, d. c.1360; m. ERIC, Duke of Södermanland in Sweden, murdered 1318 (son of Magnus I Folkung, K. of Sweden 1278–90)*

CONTINUED OVERLEAF

EUFEMIA *of Sweden, Duchess of Mecklenburg, d.1370 (sister of Magnus, K. of Norway & Sweden); m.* ALBERT I, *Duke of Mecklenburg (which had been under Danish supremacy in 13th century) d.1379*

INGEBORG *of Mecklenburg, Duchess of Slesvig, d. c.1395 (sister of Albert, K. of Sweden 1363–89); m.* HENRY II, *Count of Holstein, claimant of Danish duchy of Slesvig & lordship of Jutland, d.1384*

GERHARD VI, *Duke of Slesvig & Lord of Jutland under Denmark, Count of Holstein in Holy Roman Empire, murdered 1404*

HEDWIG *of Slesvig, Countess of Oldenburg, d.1436; m.* DIETRICH, *Count of Oldenburg, nicknamed 'Fortunatus', d.1440 (claimed descent from Saxon hero Widukind)*

CHRISTIAN I, *K. of Norway, Denmark & Sweden, d.1481 (direct male line ancestor of the Prince of Wales)*

ancestors of HRH   *See Table 36*

---

36 **SCANDINAVIA:** DENMARK & NORWAY
Skiöldungs *(Aesir)*

IVAR *'Wide-Fathom', Woden-born Skiöldung sacral K. at Lethra in Denmark, conquered sacral Uppsala in Sweden, living c.690*

AUD *(ancestress by first husband* RURIK *of Russian Grand Princes: see Table 33); m. secondly* RADBARD, *7th century saga-time*

RANDVER *(half-brother of* HARALD *Hilditönn, K. at Lethra, slain in great sea battle of Bravalla or Bravik 770)*

SIGURD *Ring, K. of Sjaelland in Denmark & Uppsala in Sweden, slew uncle K.* HARALD *at Bravik 770, d.812*

RAGNAR *'Shaggy-Breeks' (Lodbrok), Danish K. with own saga, said to have perished in Northumbrian snake-pit 845*

SIGURD II *'Dragon-Eye', Danish K., invaded England, said to have avenged father by making 'blood-eagle' of foe, d.873*

HORDA–CANUTE *(Knutr I), K. of Sjaelland in Denmark, d.884*

FROTHO, *K. of Sjaelland in Denmark, d.885 (at this period Jutland was a separate kingdom)*

HARALD II, *K. of Sjaelland in Denmark, d.899*

GORM *'the Old', K. of Denmark, under whom Sjaelland & Jutland were united, also K. of East Anglia 905–18, d.936*

HARALD III *'Blue-Tooth', K. of Denmark, established Christianity in Denmark, d.986*

SWEYN I *'Fork-Beard', K. of Denmark & England, ransomed from Jomsvikings by jewellery of Danish women, d.1014*

ASTRID *of Denmark (sister of Canute the Great, K. of Denmark, Norway & England, who d.1035); m. Jarl* ULF, *d.1028, son of Jarl* THORKILL, *son of dread pirate prince* STYRBJÖRN, *Jarl of the Jomsvikings*

SWEYN II *Astrid's-son, K. of Denmark, long at war with K.* HARALD *Haardrade of Norway, d.1076*

ERIC I *Godi, K. of Denmark, mediated between the Kings of Sweden & Norway at Konghelle 1100, d.1103*

CANUTE *(Knutr Lavardr), K. of the Obotrites, Duke of Slesvig, 'chivalrous & popular', murdered 1131*

VALDEMAR I *'the Great', K. of Denmark, cleared the Baltic of Wendish pirates, chopping up their heathen idol, d.1182*

CONTINUED OVERLEAF

Viking ship in which King Olaf Geirstadr-Alf (almost certainly ancestor of HRH) was
buried with two sacrificed women c.840. HRH also descends from his nephew Harold
Fair-Hair, first King of Norway

VALDEMAR II *'the Old', K. of Denmark, crusader in pagan Esthonia, received sacred Dannebrog flag, d.1241*

CHRISTOPHER I, *K. of Denmark, d.1259 (his bros. Valdemar III, Eric IV & Abel were each King first)*

ERIC V *Glipping, K. of Denmark, allied with Hanseatic cities against Norway, murdered by traitors 1286*

RICHSA *of Denmark, Princess of Werle, d. c.1308; m.* NICHOLAS II *of Mecklenburg, Prince of Werle, d.1316 (a Baltic Slav prince)*

SOPHIA *of Mecklenburg-Parchim, Duchess of South Jutland (Slesvig) d. c.1339; m.* GERHARD III *'the Great' of Holstein, Duke of Slesvig (uncle & guardian of K. Valdemar V), assassinated 1340*

HENRY II, *Count of Holstein, claimant of Danish duchy of Slesvig & Lordship of Jutland, d.1384*

GERHARD VI, *Duke of Slesvig & Lord of Jutland under Denmark, Count of Holstein in Holy Roman Empire, murdered 1404*

HEDWIG *of Slesvig, Countess of Oldenburg, d.1436; m.* DIETRICH, *Count of Oldenburg, nicknamed 'Fortunatus', d.1440*

CHRISTIAN I, *K. of Denmark, Norway & Sweden, pawned Orkney to Scotland (as dowry of his dau. Q.* MARGARET) *d.1481*

FREDERICK I, *K. of Denmark & Norway, chosen K. on the flight of his nephew Christian II 1523, d.1533*

CHRISTIAN III, *K. of Denmark & Norway, d.1559 (bro.* ADOLPHUS *was male-line ancestor of the later Czars of Russia)*

FREDERICK II, *K. of Denmark & Norway, 'beloved by his people', under whom Danish ships ruled Baltic, d.1588*

CHRISTIAN IV, *K. of Denmark & Norway, enlarged & embellished Copenhagen & Elsinore, d.1648*

FREDERICK III, *K. of Denmark & Norway, said 'I will die in my nest' & successfully defended Copenhagen against Swedes, d.1670*

CHRISTIAN V, *K. of Denmark & Norway, at war with Sweden, which had invaded Pomerania, d.1699*

FREDERICK IV, *K. of Denmark & Norway, abolished serfdom on royal estates, d.1730*

CHRISTIAN VI, *K. of Denmark & Norway, 'religious and benevolent', d.1746*

FREDERICK V, *K. of Denmark & Norway, promoted commerce, industry & agriculture, d.1766*

Prince FREDERICK *of Denmark, d.1805 (bro. of K. Charles VII who d.1808)*

Princess CHARLOTTE *of Denmark, d.1864 (sister of K. Christian VIII 1839–48); m. Landgrave* WILLIAM *of Hesse-Cassel, d.1867*

Landgravine LOUISE *of Hesse-Cassel, Queen of Denmark, d.1898; m.* CHRISTIAN IX, *K. of Denmark, d.1906 (male line heir of K.* CHRISTIAN III *above)*

Prince WILLIAM *of Denmark (K.* GEORGE I *of the Hellenes) assassinated 1926*

Prince ANDREW *of Greece & Denmark, d.1944*

Prince PHILIP *of Greece & Denmark (Prince* PHILIP, *Duke of Edinburgh) b.1921*

Prince CHARLES, *Prince of Wales, b.1948*

HRH

IVAR *'Wide-fathom' from Skåne, Woden-born K. at Uppsala in Sweden by conquest from its last 'peace-King', also K. of Lethra, c.690*

AUD *(m.* RADBARD, *8th century saga-time)*

RANDVER *(half-brother of* HARALD *Hilditönn, Danish K. slain in epic sea battle of Bravik 770)*

SIGURD *Ring, K. at pagan sacred Uppsala in Sweden, also K. at Lethra, victor of Bravik fight 770, d.812*

RAGNAR *'Hairy-Breeks' (Lodbrok), Danish K. at Lethra, hero of his own famous saga, attacked Paris, perished 845*

BJÖRN *Ironside, Swedish K. at Uppsala, led great Viking raid round Spain into Mediterranean in 859*

ERIC III, *Swedish K. at Uppsala, 9th century*

EYMUND, *Swedish K. at Birka, 9th century*

ERIC V, *K. of the Swedes & the Goths, authority extended as far as Norway, d.906*

BJÖRN *'the Old', Swedish K. at Uppsala, said to have reigned for 50 years, d.956*

ERIC *'the Victorious', Swedish K. at Uppsala, defeated & killed his bro. K.* OLAF's *son the Jomsviking jarl* STYRBJÖRN, *d. c.995*

OLAF *Skötkonung, first K. of all Sweden from 1001, baptised a Christian at Husaby 1008, d.1022*

EYMUND *'the Old', K. of Sweden, originally passed over because mother was unfree (a captive Slav princess), d. c.1056*

Swedish princess (m. STENKIL, *K. of Sweden 1060–6, son of* RAGNVALD, *Jarl of West Gothland)*

INGE I, *K. of Sweden, deposed 1081 by pagan K. 'Blood'* SWEYN, *who revived human sacrifice, but slew him 1083, d.1112*

Princess CATHERINE *of Sweden (m. Prince* BJÖRN *of Denmark, d.1134)*

CHRISTINA *of Denmark, Queen of Sweden; m.* ERIC IX, *K. of Sweden 1150–60 (son of* JEDWARD *by* CECILIA, *dau. of 'Blood'-*SWEYN, *last pagan K. of Sweden)*

CANUTE I *(Knut), K. of Sweden, imprisoned a pretender to Norwegian throne, who broke a hip escaping, d.1196*

ERIC X, *K. of Sweden 1208–18*

Princess INGEBORG *of Sweden, d.1254; m. Jarl* BIRGER, *Regent of Sweden 1248–66, founder of Stockholm, 'the greatest medieval statesman of Sweden' (a Folkung)*

MAGNUS I *Ladulås, K. of Sweden, made great constitutional changes & granted charter to towns, d.1290*

ERIC, *Duke of Södermanland in Sweden, murdered 1318*

EUFEMIA *of Sweden, d.1370 (m.* ALBERT I, *Duke of Mecklenburg, d.1379)*

INGEBORG *of Mecklenburg, Duchess of Slesvig, d. c.1395 (sister of Albert, K. of Sweden 1363–89); m.* HENRY II, *Count of Holstein, claimant of Danish duchy of Slesvig & lordship of Jutland, d.1384*

GERHARD VI, *Duke of Slesvig & Lord of Jutland under Denmark, Count of Holstein in Holy Roman Empire, murdered 1404*

HEDWIG *of Slesvig d.1436 (m.* DIETRICH *'Fortunatus', Count of Oldenburg, d.1440)*

CHRISTIAN I, *K. of Sweden, Denmark & Norway, temporarily united all Scandinavia, d.1481*

FREDERICK I, *K. of Denmark & Norway, d.1533 (bro. of John II, K. of Sweden 1483–1501)*

ADOLPHUS, *Duke of Slesvig-Holstein at Gottorp, d.1586*

CONTINUED OVERLEAF

CHRISTINA *of Slesvig, Queen of Sweden, d.1625; m.*
CHARLES IX *Vasa, K. of Sweden, d.1611
(son of* GUSTAVUS I *Vasa, K. of Sweden
1523–60)*

CATHERINE *of Sweden, d.1638 (sister of the great K.
Gustavus Adolphus, killed 1632, & aunt of
famous Queen Christina, d. Rome 1689); m.*
JOHN CASIMIR *of Wittelsbach, Count
Palatine of Zweibrücken, 1652*

CHARLES X, *K. of Sweden, brilliant soldier-statesman,
overcame Poland, crossed frozen Baltic to
defeat Danes, d.1660*

CHARLES XI, *K. of Sweden, one of greatest of all kings
of Sweden, as soldier & administrator,
d.1697*

HEDWIG *of Sweden (sister of the celebrated Charles
XII, K. of Sweden, killed in action 1718); m.*
FREDERICK IV, *Duke of Holstein-Gottorp,
killed in battle 1702*

CHARLES FREDERICK, *Duke of Holstein-Gottorp,
d.1739*

PETER III, *Emperor of Russia, strangled 1762*

ancestors of HRH   *See Table 34*

Crown in which HRH's ancestor King Charles IX Vasa
was buried in 1611

SCANDINAVIA

I N Scandinavia were the ancestral roots of some of
the most dynamic sacral royalty the world will
ever have seen. This is the land that formed the
sacred dynastic nucleus whence came the royal
houses of the Anglo-Saxons and Teutons and
Russians, the Merovingians of France, Visigoths of
Spain and 'Long-beards' or Lombards of Italy.

The very word 'king' (Old Norse *konungr*) is
derived from *kon*, meaning kin, with the suffix *-ung*
or *-ing* signifying descendant: i.e. 'son of *the* (sacral
royal) kindred'. Kings were simply the descendants
of the gods, that is of the dynastic families who had
ritually incarnated the god-spirits of ancient times.
The early kingship had been sacrificial, and the
royal families originally provided the ritual martyrs
who embodied the ancestral deity sacrificed 'himself to himself' at such shrines as Uppsala and
Lethra. Each temple had its king: probably, in
earlier times, his priestess-queen.

The Norse myth of the Creation held that jarl
and carl and thrall had been created separately, and
kings could only be drawn from the *genus* of jarl.

Thus the dignity of king was originally personal
rather than territorial, and all members of a royal
family were kings. This system continued perhaps
longest among the Scandinavian princes of Russia,
all of whom bore the style of *knaes*, probably
derived from the same *kn* root as *konungr*, and
among the Germans where all members of a ruling
family were counts. Thus true kings were the kin of
gods, and true princes and jarls (earls or counts)
were the kin of kings: 'there is in the earliest
Germanic times no sharp distinction between the
titles "earl" and "king".'

By the dawn of history there were, for instance,
some twenty-nine fylker or pagan local kingdoms
in Norway, with no over-king until **Harald
Fair-Hair** in the tenth century. On a local king's
death one or more of the sons remained in the
family *fylke*, to perform the priestly sacrifices in its
temple and to be its battle-leaders, while the other
sons took their share of the fortune and set out with
a band of warrior-companions (the *hird*, equivalent
of the Welsh *teulu* and Russian *druzhina*, who never

left a battlefield without their king, dead or alive), to become roving sea-kings or else acquire land by conquest or marriage to the heiress of some outland temple, to be their kingdom elsewhere. This is the epoch of the princes in fairy tales. The sagas reveal strong traces of matrilinear succession in ancient times, coupled with the slaying of the king's predecessor by conquerors qualified by royal birth: a well-known feature of so many pagan sacral kingships in other parts of the world.

At the time of their conversion to Christianity during the tenth century, the chief royal houses of the Northmen were the various branches of two great dynasties: the **Skiöldungs** and **Ynglings**. We understand from the sagas that the **Skiöldungs**

Christian I, King of Denmark, Norway and Sweden died 1481, and his wife Dorothea of Hohenzollern, daughter of John, Margrave of Brandenburg. HRH's ancestors in the direct male line

belonged to the semi-divine family of the *Aesir* and were originally the pagan sacral dynasty whose sacred capital was Lethra (Lejre) on the Danish island of Sjaelland and who claimed descent from Skiöldr or Scyld, son of the god Woden, i.e. from kings who had ritually incarnated the storm-spirit Woden (known as Vata as far afield as Vedic India) after whom Wednesday is named; while the **Ynglings** belonged to the rival semi-divine family of the *Vanir* and were originally the pagan sacral dynasty known as the 'Peace Kings of Uppsala' who claimed descent from Frey son of Niördr, the male embodiment through Freya of the ancient goddess Nerthus, the spirit of 'Mother Earth' (Frey simply means Our Lord and Freya, Our Lady), after whom Friday is named. In Norse mythology, the *Aesir* and *Vanir* first fought one another among the gods but then were reconciled. In real life, the same is true of their sacral royal descendants.

Indeed, the main difficulty lies in disentangling the two dynasties before the end of the ninth century, for they were much inter-married and reigned in different generations in the same kingdom as each other: so that it is not absolutely certain in all cases which dynasty was which, especially in Ireland, at York and in the Hebrides. But, after the ninth century, the **Skiöldungs** reigned in Denmark, Sweden and probably in Russia, while the **Ynglings** reigned in Norway, Orkney, Normandy and probably also in Dublin, Waterford, Limerick, the Isle of Man and the Hebrides. The Anglo-Saxon and Danish kings of all England (though not all the local Anglo-Saxon and Anglo-Danish dynasts) were **Skiöldungs** (Scyldings), and the Norman kings of England, as also **Strongbow** (leader of the Anglo-Norman invasion of Ireland), were **Ynglings**. HRH descends from all these dynasties, the last pagan sacral king of which was **Sweyn, King of Sweden** (slain by **King Inge** I in 1083) known as **Blot-Sweyn** from his revival of the ancient human sacrifices.

This is explained in my book *Blood Royal*: 'The early food-producers perceived divine power in the life-force which impregnated matter with energy. They saw this as the marriage of Sky and Earth. The hereditary queen incarnated the power in Mother Earth, and at her sacred marriage her king was identified with the power in Sun and Sky. The beneficent spirits inhabiting divine royalty were not thought omnipotent. But they were the first gods.' Here the word 'god' must be understood as 'spirit' almost in the sense of lucky mascots, and in modern times has become allegorical, just as our anointed Queen could be said to embody the Spirit of Britannia. 'Moreover, loss of bodily vigour in such a king seemed pregnant with disaster to the community – for the precious Spirit might be impaired. So the king sacrificed himself, and was ritually slain before loss of virility.' The local spirit of good luck was given a new body of the Blood Royal – in the earliest times probably by the new king eating part of the old king and drinking his blood in a symbolic communion. Just as a new matrilinear queen was born out of the old queen, the old king literally went into the new king. 'Later, royal princes or other sacrificial substitutes for the king's own flesh and blood were provided – human, animal or vegetable – by ritual that infused them with royalty before sacrifice. From the ancient ritual of the king dying for his people, the idea of sacrifice pervaded early religion.'

Thus the **Peace Kings of Uppsala** appear to have been long established, when Tacitus wrote about the Swedes (Suiones) c. 98 AD that their king had so mighty a fleet that home defence was unnecessary, so that in times of peace all weapons were stored away. There was a splendid heathen temple at Uppsala, built of wood but 'gleaming with gold', and beside it a sacred grove where stood a particularly venerated tree on which the sacrificed bodies were hanged. Here the Great Mother had been worshipped under the name of Nerthus, whose place was taken in later times by her male equivalent Niördr, incarnate in his 'son' Frey, the spirit ritually embodied in each living king, 'whose reign was marked by the Frith Frothi, the Peace of Freyr, which secured the fruitfulness of the earth and of men. The centre of his cult was the great sanctuary at Uppsala, where his ithyphallic image was placed, and whence, like Nerthus, he was carried forth in a waggon through the land accompanied by a priestess who was his human spouse.' Every nine years, the king himself was sacrificed, until we learn that HRH's then semi-legendary forefather, *King Aun the Old*, offered up one of his own sons as a substitute every ninth year. But when there was only one son left, to save the dynasty the people sacrificed *Aun* himself: his great grave mound being one of the three ancient barrows still pointed out at Uppsala.

This dynasty were called **Ynglings** probably after **King Yngvarr**, son of *King Eystein I* (Östen), son of *King Athils* (Eadgils) whose ancestral first cousin was King Hugleik (Hygelac). Here we are in the realm where saga and epic poem and history meet: for in HRH's ancestor *King Athils* we see the *King Eadgils of the Swedes* whom his kinsman the epic hero Beowulf enthroned by force of arms; and in their mutual relation King Hugleik (Hygelac) can recognise the Scandinavian king of that name slain in a naval battle against the Franks c. 515 in the mouth of the Rhine, where his gigantic skeleton was still exhibited as a curiosity on an island as late as the tenth century. Moreover, in the 'Beowulf' poem HRH's **Ynglingar** forefathers are called the Swedish Scylfingar, which corresponds with the name **Skilfingar** by which they are sometimes also known in the sagas. However, **King Yngvarr's** grandson, **King Ingiald 'Ill-Ruler'**, was last of the **Peace Kings of Uppsala**, whence he was driven towards the close of the seventh century by a Skiöldung royalty from Skåne, the famous **Ivar 'Wide-Fathom'**, after which images of Odin or Woden and Thor were placed beside that of Frey in the temple of Uppsala. It may have been then that royal hanging was also introduced there as the method of sacrifice.

For **King Ivar 'Wide-Fathom'** was Woden-born, being also king at hallowed Lethra where there is a sacred stone circle on the Danish island of Sjaelland, and ate horse-flesh at the Yuletide sacrifice. In early times, his **Skiöldung** dynasty were also hereditary martyrs, for their incarnation of Woden evidently entailed being sacrificed in due time by hanging on a sacred ash tree (hanging gives an erection, symbol of fertility) and being speared

so that royal blood fell to the ground: remember for instance Odin's words in the Hávamál poem in the Verse Edda, 'myself a sacrifice to myself'. In this connection, it's perhaps worth noting the nobility of feature of the ancient man (possibly one of HRH's royal ancestors) found ritually hanged, his body having been preserved by the Tollund bog in Jutland; and that the regalia inherited by the Wessex branch of the House of Woden included a sacred spear, known in Christian times as the spear from Calvary, and given as a holy relic by King Athelstan to his brother-in-law, the **Emperor Otto**. When dying abed by mischance, members of the Skiöldung family were 'marked unto Odin' by wounding with a spear-point, and Norse dynasts sought 'death by weapon' so as to be claimed as his own by Woden in Valhalla.

NORWAY

Hᴿᴴ's Norwegian forefathers were so adventurous that it's hard to single out any particular Viking for special mention. But the country was first united by King **Harald 'Thick-Hair'** or **'Fair-Hair'** (died 934), so called because a princess whose hand he had asked made him vow not to cut his hair until he had conquered all the nigh on thirty fjord kingdoms that made up Norway. This he did, after which his blond hair was trimmed.

And the English will always remember **King Harald Haardrade**, who ended up with six feet of English ground (or a bit more, as he was taller than other men) when he was slain with his ally **Earl Tostig** while invading England in 1066, when surprised at Stamford Bridge by **Tostig**'s brother, the Anglo-Saxon Scylding **King Harold**, himself so soon afterwards killed at Hastings by the Norman Yngling **Duke William the Conqueror**. The famous sacred 'Lord-Ravager' flag that **King Harald Haardrade of Norway** had brought back

from his days as Captain of the Varangian Guard at Constantinople, which gave its owner victory in battle but which he is known to have left behind that fatal day with the ships in which **Godred Crovan** (afterwards **King of Man and the Isles**) escaped, is very probably now the celebrated Fairy Flag of the MacLeod chiefs who, like HRH, descend from **King Godred** – himself probably a descendant of **King Harald Fair-hair**'s half-brother *King Olaf Geirstadr-Alf*. Certainly the Fairy Flag is of 'oriental Mediterranean silken fabric, more than a thousand years old, and very carefully stitched in the darns: possibly a saint's shirt kept to bear in peace or war as a lucky relic.'

Later, Norway joined up with Denmark from the fifteenth until the nineteenth century and, after a brief union with Sweden, became separate again in 1905 with its present royal family, chosen from the same Danish dynasty as HRH's grandfather **Prince Philip, Duke of Edinburgh.**

DENMARK

AGAIN, it's difficult to single out particular kings among the Danes. HRH's ancestral uncle, King Canute the Great of Denmark and England, will always be remembered for his gesture to reprove the courtier who suggested he could control the tides: though the story that has come down to us may be a garbled version of some ancient ritual.

King Valdemar the Old, who codified the Danish laws, greatly extended Danish power in the Baltic by leading a crusade against the pagan Esthonians, and, when treacherously attacked in his camp near Reval after they had pretended to submit, was saved, we are told, by the miraculous descent from heaven of a red banner with a white cross on it: the famous Dannebrog (Danes' Cloth), which became the national flag. Soon **Valdemar** had extended the Danish empire from the Elbe to Lake Peipus. Then suddenly, in 1223, during a hunting party on an island, he was kidnapped at midnight from his tent by his own guest and vassal Count Henry of Schwerin, who carried him off to a castle on the Elbe, whence he was only ransomed with the loss of much territory two and a half years later; and at the decisive battle of Bornhöved in 1227, **Valdemar** was heavily defeated in his attempt to restore Danish hegemony in the eastern Baltic.

Famous Danish names in HRH's ancestry include the Houses of **Königsmark** and **Raben, Rantzau** and **Reventlow**, also **Frederick, Count of Ahlefeldt** (died 1686). But HRH's Danish ancestry reaches the twentieth century. Under **Christian I, King of Denmark** 1448–81, all Scandinavia had been briefly united. And he was forefather of HRH in the direct male line, through **Christian IX, King of Denmark** 1863–1906, and **Prince Philip, Duke of Edinburgh**, who was of course born a **Prince of Denmark.**

SWEDEN

VERY few Swedes realise that their own present royal family, like HRH, descend (in their case through the Margraves of Baden) from the **Peace Kings of Uppsala** in ancient times and the **Skiöldung Kings of Sweden** in saga-time, by way of that great **Folkung** regent, **Birger Jarl**, who founded Stockholm in the thirteenth century, and the mighty Houses of **Vasa** and **Wittelsbach** in Sweden's greatest days.

But HRH also descends from **Carl Knutsson Bonde, King of Sweden** as **Charles VIII** (died 1470), and from the noble Swedish families who administered the realm under the title of 'Riksförestandare' during the difficult years at the end of the fifteenth and beginning of the sixteenth century: from **Kristiern Bengtsson Oxenstjerna** whose brother **Jons** was **Riksförestandare** 1465–6, from **Lars Axelsson Tott** whose brother **Erik** held that position 1466–7, from **Svante Nilsson Sture, Riksförestandare** 1504–12 and from **Sten Svantesson Sture, Riksförestandare** 1512–20. The next Rikförestandare was elected king as **Gustavus I Vasa, King of Sweden** 1523–60, the genius who became one of Sweden's greatest monarchs.

Other famous names among HRH's ancestors in Sweden's mighty days are **Bielke** and **Banér, Gyllenstjerna** and **Leijonhufvud** and **Trolle**: and indeed HRH's forefather **Count Bengt Oxenstjerna** (died 1702), the famous foreign minister and co-Regent of Sweden, was nephew of Sweden's great and wise Chancellor, Count Axel Oxenstjerna (died 1654), who succeede HRH's other ancestral uncle King Gustavus Adolphus as effective ruler of the realm in Sweden's Golden Age.

HRH's Swedish royal ancestry comes down from **Princess Hedwig of Sweden**, sister of the celebrated King Charles XII who 'went to Russia by way of Poltava', and daughter of **Charles XI, King of Sweden** 1660–7, of whom it was said that the Swedish people, 'knowing the king to be their best friend, trusted him implicitly and co-operated with him cheerfully'.

Battle saddlery of HRH's ancestral uncle King Gustavus Adolphus, killed in action 1632

THE CID *(Rodrigo Diaz de Bivar, el Campeador), epic hero of Spain, d.1099*

ELVIRA *(Christina) of Bivar, m.* RAMIRO II, *Count of Maçon, d.1116*

GARCIA VI *el Restaurador, K. of Navarre, country of Basques and Gascons, d.1150*

BLANCA *of Navarre d.1158, m.* SANCHO III, *K. of Castile, d.1158 (sprung in the female line from* BERMUDO, *K. of Asturias, d.792)*

ALFONSO VIII *the Noble, K. of Castile, led the coalition that broke power of Moorish Almohades, d.1214*

BERENGARIA *of Castile d.1244, m.* ALFONSO IX *the Slobberer, K. of Leon, foamed at the mouth in fits of rage, d.1230*

St FERNANDO III, *K. of Castile & Leon, canonised, conquered Cordoba & Seville from Moors, d.1252*

ALFONSO X *the Sage, K. of Castile & Leon, titular German King of the Romans, keen astronomer, d.1284*

SANCHO IV *the Brave, K. of Castile & Leon, conquered Tarifa from Moors, d.1296*

FERNANDO IV *el Emplazado 'the Summoned', K. of Castile & Leon, protected by Avila citizens as a boy, d.1312*

ALFONSO XI *the Avenger, K. of Castile & Leon, defeated last great Moorish invasion of Spain, d. of Black Death 1350*

PEDRO *the Cruel, K. of Castile & Leon, murdered many, but was slain by his natural bro. K.* HENRY *of Trastamara*

CONSTANCE *of Castile & Leon, d.1394; m.* JOHN, *Duke of Lancaster, titular K. of Castile & Leon, d.1399*

The Infantes of Carrion humiliate their newly-wed wives, the daughters of the Cid, from the *Crónica del Cid*

CONSTANCE *of Lancaster & Castile, d.1418; m.* ENRIQUE III *(Henry the Sufferer), K. of Castile & Leon, d.1406 (grandson of K.* HENRY *of Trastamara)*

JUAN II, *K. of Castile & Leon, philosopher and poet, encouraged literature, enjoyed tournaments, d.1454*

ISABELLA, *Queen of Castile & Leon, d.1504; m.* FERNANDO, *K. of Aragon & Sicily, d.1516 (they sent Columbus to discover America)*

JUANA *la Loca (the Mad), Queen of Spain, d.1555, refused for a long time to be parted from her husband's corpse; m.* PHILIP I *the Fair, K. Consort of Spain (Archduke of Austria) 1504–6*

Emperor FERDINAND I, *d.1564 (bro. of Emperor Charles V, K. of Spain, ruler from Vienna to Peru)*

▲ *ancestors of* HRH *See Tables 7 & 29*

SPAIN

THE great Spanish royal and noble houses were doubtless of grand Visigothic origin, but their detailed pedigrees from the kindred of the pagan sacral kings was lost, not only in their adoption of Christianity under late Roman influence, but in the long struggle to save at first the remnant, and then recover the rest, of Spain from the domination of Islam.

For in 711, HRH's distinguished Arab ancestor – (through **Zadan Zada, lord of Gaya**, and the houses of **Albohazar**, **de Maya** and **Meneses**) – **Musa ibn Nosayr el-Bekri, Viceroy of Ifrikiqia**, which was Moslem north Africa from Tripoli to Morocco, sent his general Tariq (after whom Gibraltar or Jebel Tariq, the 'Rock of Tariq', is named) across the Straits of Gibraltar to defeat the Visigoths, and by 712 **Musa** himself arrived with a large army of conquest as **Viceroy of Spain**. Despite the great booty, especially of valued blonde maidens for the harems of Syria, the Caliph was not grateful to so over-mighty a subject; and the great **Viceroy Musa ibn Nosayr** died, aged over eighty, a prisoner in Damascus. Equally, **Musa**'s son **Abd el-Aziz ibn Musa**, whom he had left behind as **Viceroy of Spain**, was in his turn decapitated in the mosque at Seville in 717 and his pickled head sent to appease the jealous Caliph.

Meanwhile, the Visigothic nobles still held out in the Cantabrian Mountains of northern Spain. **Pedro, Duke in Calabria**, had two sons, Alfonso, who became King of Asturias in 739, and **Count Fruela**, who held out in what later became known as Castile: the gradually conquered 'land of castles'. **Count Fruela**'s son **Bermudo I, King of Asturias** 788–91, was ancestor of HRH and indeed of all the future Spanish kings. Out of these steel-hardened royal warriors, fighting as crusaders to retain or regain their own soil from the Sword of Islam, there emerged HRH's various forefathers who founded and eventually united the separate Kingdoms of Leon, Galicia, Aragon and Castile; also the **Kings of Navarre**, the **Counts of Barcelona** in Catalonia (descended from the Frankish **count Wilfred the Hairy**), the mighty **Lords of Biscay**, the celebrated **Infantes de Lara** and the famous **House of Guzman** (itself sprung from a younger brother of **King Bermudo**). These were heroic days, and there is even a traditional descent in the female line from **Charlemagne**'s immortal paladin *Roland*, whose great horn has echoed down the centuries from the Pass of Roncesvalles. He was in fact *Hruodland*, Praefect of the Breton March, slain in 778 when the Frankish rearguard was ambushed in the Pyrenees by the Basques.

But these heroic days were strenuous and tough, and the Byzantine Christian method of blinding instead of execution was sometimes resorted to when settling dynastic problems. Thus **Ramiro II, King of Leon** 931–50, 'came to the throne after putting out the eyes of all the nearest of his relations, and won what is admitted to be a decisive victory over the Moors at Simancas'. **Ramiro**'s son, **King Ordoño III**, married **Urraca**, daughter of the famous **Fernan Gonsalez, Count of Castile**, hero of many a Castilian ballad; but when the great Count quarrelled with the next king, he set up against him one of the poor old blinded princes, locked away since **Ramiro**'s accession a quarter of a century before. The kingdoms of Castile, Aragon and Navarre were briefly united under **King Sancho the Great**, but unfortunately, at his death in 1035 they were divided again among his sons.

In the following century, another epic hero, appears in HRH's ancestry many times over. This was **the Cid**, from the name 'el Said' meaning 'the lord' given him out of respect by the Moors, also called **el Campeador** (the champion) by the Spaniards as he slew the champion of **King Sancho IV of Navarre** in single combat while acting as personal champion of King Sancho II of Castile, brother of the future **King Alfonso VI**. The real name of **the Cid** was **Rodrigo Diaz de Bivar** (his Christian name being the then form of the old Visigothic name Roderic) and he too could be pretty rough: when he took the rich Moorish city of Valencia in 1094 after a siege of nine months, he had the unjust 'qadi' or supreme judge burnt alive at the stake, despite a promise of safety, when he was proved guilty of a previous crime. On the other hand, he proclaimed to the Moorish population: 'I am a man who never possessed a kingdom, but from the day I first came to this city, I set my heart on it, and now God in his mercy has given me Valencia and made me its master. If I order its affairs justly and deal fairly, God will leave it in my hands; but if I deal ill, He will take it from me. From today, therefore, each one of you may go to his property and enjoy it as he was used ... if any of your complaints are urgent, come to me on any day and I will hear you ... I want to interest myself in your affairs, to be for you as a companion, to protect you as a friend protects a friend and a relative his relative. 'I wish to be for you both *qadi* who judges and *vizier* who governs; and when you quarrel, I will always see that justice is done.' And he ruled his kingdom of Valencia and Murcia justly until his death four years later from an old spear wound.

In 1235, HRH's forefather **Saint Fernando, King of united Castile & Leon** and canonised after his death, reconquered Cordoba, the splendid capital of the Moslem caliphate itself, soon to be followed by Seville; while about the same time Valencia was retaken from the Moors by another of HRH's greatest ancestors, the gigantic, nearly seven foot tall, **Jaime el Conquistador, King of Aragon** 1213–76, a long and victorious reign of sixty-three years, who had already recovered Majorca from the Barbary corsairs. He had inherited the throne as a boy when his father, **King Pedro II**, was slain at Muret attempting to support the Albigenses' acknowledged protector **Raymond-Roger, Count of Foix** and rightful **Vicomte of Béziers**, in giving generous help to the unfortunate Albigenses, whose secret Cathar form of Christianity has been linked to the cult of the Holy Grail, and against whom the stern northerner **Simon IV de Montfort, Vicomte of Béziers and Carcassone** by ruthless conquest (father of the celebrated English parliamentarian), was leading an implacable 'crusade'; the leaders on both sides being HRH's direct ancestors. **King Jaime el Conquistador** has left us his own autobiography, written in Catalan 'in a simple, manly style, with obvious sincerity of purpose': of his father's death he wrote 'Thus died my father, for such has ever been the fate of my race, to conquer or to die in battle.'

When **Alfonso X the Sage, King of Castile**, 'the first monarch of modern Europe who was also a man of letters' and who had claimed vainly to be German King as maternal grandson of the **Emperor Philip of Hohenstaufen**, died in 1284, his rebellious second son **Sancho IV** succeeded him as king in preference to the baby children of his eldest son the **Infante Fernando de la Cerda** (so called from a tuft of hair, 'cerda', growing out of a mole on his face), who had died in 1275. HRH descends from both sons, about whom a curious custom arose: 'The **La Cerdas**, as representatives of the elder son of **Alfonso X**, never ceased to urge their claims to the crown. Long after they had become reconciled to the throne, the head of their house, on the accession of a new king, would put in an appearance and formally claim the title, for which he would be fined in a nominal sum. The farce was kept up down to 1808.'

HRH descends also from many of the other famous families that took part in the liberation of the land from the Moors and its forging into the single realm. Those ancestors included **Don Pedro Ruiz de Guzman** (uncle of St Dominic, who died in 1221, founder of the Dominican preaching friars or Black Friars), **Don Pedro Gonsalez de Mendoza, Grand Chamberlain of Castile**, slain at Aljubarrota in 1385, **Don Pedro Alvarez Osorio 'el Bueno'** (the Good), who inherited the **Quiñones** lordship in 1388, the bearers of such great Spanish names as **Ayala**, the **Enriquez** hereditary admirals of Castile, **Luna**, **Pimentel**, **Ponce de Leon**, **Sandoval**, the **Tellez de Meneses counts of Leiva** (with their celebrated plain golden shield and banner, bearing no device), **Hurtado de Mendoza** and **Velasco**; also, rather unexpectedly, **Don Juan de Pacheco, Marques of Villena & Duke of Escalona**, Grand Master of the Military Order of Santiago, who died in 1474, at first the royal favourite and then the leader of the insurgent nobles against King Henry the Impotent of Castile.

Among the greatest of HRH's Spanish ancestors (through the Spencers' descents from the Medici) was **Don Pedro Alvarez de Toledo y Zuñiga, Marques of Villafranca**, Viceroy of Naples and Spanish Captain General in Italy 1532–53, brother of the famous Duke of Alba whose stern government of the Netherlands drove the Dutch into revolt, and son of **Fadrique, 2nd Duke of Alba**, Grandee of Spain and Knight of the Golden Fleece, Viceroy of Castile and Grand Chamberlain to Emperor Charles V at the height of Spanish world power.

But the most famous of all HRH's Spanish ancestors, to the English-speaking world, were **Ferdinand and Isabella, King and Queen of Castile & Aragon**, who added a pomegranate as a pun to their coat-of-arms when they conquered Granada with its beautiful Alhambra and expelled the Moors from a Spain that was re-united at last. For it was they who sent Christopher Columbus on his epoch-making voyage of discovery to the New World.

King Ferdinand and Queen Isabella, 'Los Reyes
Catolicos', who sent Columbus to the discovery of
America in 1492

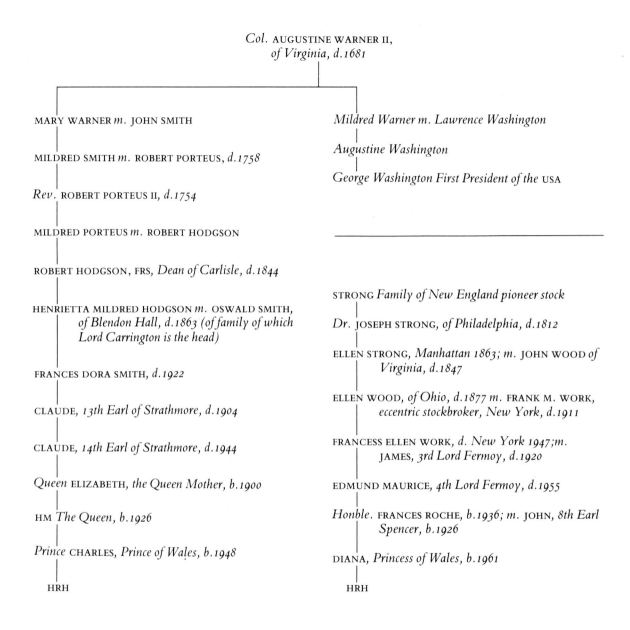

Col. AUGUSTINE WARNER II,
of Virginia, d.1681

MARY WARNER *m.* JOHN SMITH

MILDRED SMITH *m.* ROBERT PORTEUS, *d.1758*

Rev. ROBERT PORTEUS II, *d.1754*

MILDRED PORTEUS *m.* ROBERT HODGSON

ROBERT HODGSON, FRS, *Dean of Carlisle, d.1844*

HENRIETTA MILDRED HODGSON *m.* OSWALD SMITH,
*of Blendon Hall, d.1863 (of family of which
Lord Carrington is the head)*

FRANCES DORA SMITH, *d.1922*

CLAUDE, *13th Earl of Strathmore, d.1904*

CLAUDE, *14th Earl of Strathmore, d.1944*

Queen ELIZABETH, *the Queen Mother, b.1900*

HM *The Queen, b.1926*

Prince CHARLES, *Prince of Wales, b.1948*

HRH

Mildred Warner m. Lawrence Washington

Augustine Washington

George Washington First President of the USA

STRONG *Family of New England pioneer stock*

Dr. JOSEPH STRONG, *of Philadelphia, d.1812*

ELLEN STRONG, *Manhattan 1863; m.* JOHN WOOD *of
Virginia, d.1847*

ELLEN WOOD, *of Ohio, d.1877 m.* FRANK M. WORK,
eccentric stockbroker, New York, d.1911

FRANCESS ELLEN WORK, *d. New York 1947;m.*
JAMES, *3rd Lord Fermoy, d.1920*

EDMUND MAURICE, *4th Lord Fermoy, d.1955*

Honble. FRANCES ROCHE, *b.1936; m.* JOHN, *8th Earl
Spencer, b.1926*

DIANA, *Princess of Wales, b.1961*

HRH

UNITED STATES OF AMERICA

HRH had an American great-great-grandmother, **Frances Ellen Work, Lady Fermoy**, who died in 1947. A year ago, Stephen Cook wrote in the *Guardian* about her as a black sheep: '**Frances**, daughter of the eccentric **Mr. Frank Work** of New York, who wisely chose the career of stockbroker to the Vanderbilt family and amassed a large fortune. **Mr. Work** strongly disapproved of the contemporary syndrome of American money marrying in to European aristocracy, and threatened to disinherit any of his children who gave into it. **Frances** immediately defied him by marrying **James Boothby Burke Roche, heir to the second Baron Fermoy**, a family of impeccable Irish blood but uncertain fortune. Eleven years later in 1891, **Frances** was back in New York, divorcing her aristocratic husband, and asking her father to relent and take her back with her three children. **Mr. Work** did so, but made a will saying they would only inherit providing they changed their name back to Work, promised never to go to Europe for more than a holiday, and generally promised to be good Americans. Things appeared to go swimmingly until **Mr. Work** discovered, four years before he died in 1911, that **Frances** was running around with Mr. Auriel Botanyi, who was not only from Romania, but did work connected with horses. She married him and there was another row. After **Mr. Work** died, a disappointed man, his grandson, **Frances**'s eldest son **Edmund Maurice**, promptly broke the terms of the old man's will by climbing aboard the *Lusitania*, crossing to England, and standing in line for the **Fermoy** title, which he duly inherited in 1920.'

It's not within the scope of this book to point out distant cousinhoods (such as that Charles Darwin was ancestral fifth cousin of HRH), but it seems interesting in this case that the blood relationship of the **Princess of Wales** to **Prince Charles** – seventh cousin once removed, through **the 3rd Duke of Devonshire** (died 1755) – is almost exactly the same as her blood relationship – seventh cousin twice removed – to the American film star Humphrey Bogart: their common ancestor being **Joseph Morgan**, who died in 1709 in New England.

However, it is remarkable that, out of all the thousands of million people in the world, HRH should be among the nearest living relations of George Washington, first President of the USA and in a sense Father of the American Nation. The great President had no children, but he was ancestral second cousin of **Queen Elizabeth the Queen Mother** through their joint descent from the **Virginian colonel Augustine Warner** (1643–81), whose daughter was George Washington's grandmother; and whose sister incidentally, was ancestress of General Robert E. Lee. Here, HRH has two of the greatest American blood relationships.

OVERLEAF   George Washington, of whom HRH is among the nearest living relations

SOURCES OF ILLUSTRATIONS

Illustrations are reproduced by courtesy of the following: Pietro Annigoni (photograph Camera Press), p.47 bottom; Ashmolean Museum, Oxford, p.27; BBC Hulton Picture Library, pp. 59, 73, 88, 99 & 104; Bildarchiv Preussischer Kulturbeistz, Berlin, pp.80 & 81 bottom; Bodleian Library, Oxford, 35 bottom; Bran Castle, Transylvania, p.63; Bridgeman Art Library, pp.31 top & bottom, 43, and 47 top & bottom; British Library, p.71; British Museum, pp.25 and 30 bottom; copyright Broadlands (Romsey) Ltd., Romsey, Hampshire, pp.82 and 106; Camera Press, p.18; The Devonshire Collection, Chatsworth, portrait by Sir Joshua Reynolds, p.46; Christie's, p.47 top; Colour Library International, title page and p.7; Commissioners of Public Works, Ireland, p.16; The Master and Fellows of Corpus Christi College, Cambridge p.23; the Courtauld Institute of Art, pp.67, 68 and 98; Sonia Halliday (stained glass windows in Canterbury Cathedral), pp.34 & 35 top, and 58; Copyright by Interfoto MTI, Hungary, p.83;

Kunsthistorisches Museum, Vienna, p.74; Livrustkammaren, Stockholm, pp.114 and 119; Mansell Collection Ltd., pp.9, 41 and 93; Matandaran Library, Erivan, USSR, p.50; His Grace The Duke of Marlborough, p.43; Private Collection, p.24; Museo del Prado, p.121; National Museums of Antiquities of Scotland, p.22; National Museum of Wales, Cardiff, pp.12 and 13; National Portrait Gallery, London, pp.42, 43 bottom, 45 and 66; Nationalhistoriske Museum på Frederiksborg, Denmark, p.115; Novosti Press Agency, p.107 top and bottom; Rijksmuseum-Stichting, Amsterdam, portrait by T. Key, p.92; Scala/Florence, p.87; Scottish National Portrait Gallery, p. 26; Scottish Tourist Board, Edinburgh, p.11; B.A. Seaby Ltd., p.81 top; The Board of Trinity College Dublin, p.15; University Museum of National Antiquities, Oslo, Norway, p.111; Collection Viollet, pp.39 and 72 bottom; and Western American Picture Library, portrait by James Peale, p.126.